THE CLASSIC IN WAGNER

THE CLASSIC IN WAGNER

A Search for the Ring of the

Nibelung in the Iliad

Teresa Rondon Rota

To order additional copies of this book, contact:
Xlibris Corporation
1-888-795-4274
www.Xlibris.com
Orders@Xlibris.com
37077

CONTENTS

LIST OF TABLES

LIST OF FIGURES

In memoriam
To my mother and my sister Mercedes

FOREWORD

Teresa Rondón Rota may confess herself a Wagnerian with the same naturalness with which Neruda confessed himself as having lived. You cannot but pay attention to such a cultivated, tenacious, and passionate music lover, who has attended—but this is only an example—nine complete representations of the Tetralogy, when she says to have discovered in Wagner's texts and music a little-analyzed facet of his creativity, and writes a book to prove it.

As the author herself makes sure to clarify, this is not a discovery in the absolute sense of the word. Wagner himself, and more recently two of his work's *exegetas* whom she quotes, has highlighted the same facet, one of whose aspects she decides to explore in depth and in great detail. Richard Wagner's stereotype, in the minds of most of us, is that of a creator who rebels against the old and already-worn-out mythologies and who vehemently denies contemporary drama in order to, in a gesture of romantic extremism, build a theater and a national opera with a new mark of his personality, capable of emphatically expressing the spirit of the German people through Germanic myths and, above all, through a new music. But even as he worked on his revolution that led him to delve for decades into the symbology of the Germanic Nibelung saga, Wagner—and here comes the precision—never stopped being a cultivated *mitteleuropean*, imbued of that classical Greek culture translated by him during his adolescence and constantly reread during his middle age. The new Wagnerian universe of situations, characters, episodes, and even literary-musical procedures considered unprecedented can, in fact, be translated as a juxtaposition of the two cultures, as a double resonance in which the new Wotan, Brünnhilde, and Siegfried continue in some way to incarnate the conception of the world and certain expressive turns of the Homeric Zeus, Helen, and Achilles. The substance of the present work deals with this fluctuation in classic reminiscenses, some perhaps probable, others of undiscussed evidence.

It is for the readers to reach their own conclusions, which, I dare think, may be reduced to two large groups: those who would preferably underline the unending and fruitful contaminatio or mestizaje between cultures, which is always a cumulative process of the new synthesizing the old; or those who would find in this book an alternate proof: that in all of humanity's great myths and sagas—even those of disparate cultures that have never met, such as the Homeric and the Nibelungian—it is possible to find the recurrence of the same symbols obsessions, phantoms, and wishes of humanity.

Antonio Pasquali (*)

* UNESCO's ex-underdirector general for communications, author of numerous works on communications and cultural policies.

THE RING OF THE NIBELUNG

Synopsis
Table I (4)

TETRALOGY MODE OF USE

CHARACTERS according to their first appearance in scene	THE RHINEGOLD (Scenes 1-4)	THE WALKYRIE (1 Act 1-3 / 2nd Act 1-5 / 3rd Act 1-3)	SIEGFRIED (1 Act 1-3 / 2nd Act 1-3 / 3rd Act 1-3)	THE TWILIGHT OF THE GODS (PRELUDE / 1 Act 1-3 / 2nd Act 1-5 / 3rd Act 1-3)
The Rhine maidens — Woglinde (sopr.), Wellgunde (mezzo), Flosshilde (contr.) — Nymphes guardians of the gold of the Rhine	■ (sc. 1, 4)			■ (3rd Act)
Alberich (bant.) Hideous dwarf, king of the black gnomes Nibelungs, race of dwarves who inhabit the caves and are very good forgers.	■ (sc. 1, 3)		■ (2nd Act)	■ (1 Act)
Fricka (mezz.) Goddess of marriage, wife of Wotan, childless; sister of Freia, Donner and Froh.	■ (sc. 2)	■ (2nd Act)		
Wotan (the Traveller) (bant.) King of the Gods, father of nine Walkyries whose mother is Erda, the earth mother. He is also father of Siegmund and Sieglinde. He is Fricka's husband.	■ (sc. 2, 4)	■ (2nd Act, 3rd Act)	■ (1 Act, 3rd Act)	
Freia (sopr.) Goddess of abundance and love, sister of Fricka, Donner and Froh.	■ (sc. 2)			
Fasolt (bant.) One of the Giants contracted by Wotan to build the palace of the Gods: Walhall.	■ (sc. 2)			
Fafner (the Dragon) (base) the other giant who built Walhall, and who in Siegfried transforms himself into a Dragon.	■ (sc. 2)		■ (2nd Act)	
Froh (tenor) God of Happiness, brother of Donner, Fricka and Freia	■ (sc. 2)			
Donner (bant.) God of Thunder, brother of Fricka, Freia and Froh.	■ (sc. 2)			
Loge (tenor) God of Fire, of Flames, and also of the Ruse and the Lie, astute and harmful.	■ (sc. 2)	■ (3rd Act)	■ (1 Act)	
Mime (tenor) Dwarf or Nibelung, blacksmith, adoptive father of Siegfried but hated by him, who kills him	■ (sc. 3)		■ (1 Act)	
Erda (contr.) God of Wisdom and of the Earth Mother of the Norns and the Walkyries whose father...	■ (sc. 4)		■ (3rd Act)	

(side label: THE RHINEGOLD *)*

After Albert Lavignac,
Le Voyage artistique à Bayreuth,
Editions Delagrave, Paris, 1900

THE WALKYRIE

Siegmund (tenor) Wotan's son (under the name of Waelse), brother and husband of Sieglinde, father of Siegfried.

Sieglinde (sopr.) Daughter of Wotan (under name of Waelse), wife of Hunding, later of Siegmund, her brother, mother of Siegfried

Hunding (base) First husband to Sieglinde, who detests him, because she had been sold to him.

Brünnhilde (sopr.) The oldest of the Walkyries, daughter of Wotan and Erda, wife of Siegfried, after of Gunther by treason.

The Walkyries { Helmwige, Guerhilde (sopr.) Waltraute (mezz.) Ortlinde, Siegrune, Rossweisse (mezz.) Grimguerde, Schwertleite (contr.) } Warriors, daughters of Wotan and Erda, sisters of Brünnhilde.

SIEGFRIED

Siegfried (tenor) Son of Segmund and Sieglinde, grandson of Wotan (Waelse), husband of Brünnhilde, later husband of Gutrune (sister of Gunther) by treason.

The Bird (sopr.) Personage prophetic and misterious.

THE TWILIGHT OF THE GODS

The Norns { 1st. Norn (contr.) 2nd. Norn (mezz.) 3rd. Norn (sopr.) } { Daughters of the Earth, who know the destiny of the Gods and of the humans, and know the future.

Gunther (barit.) Son of Gilbich and Grimhilde, brother of Gutrune, half brother of Hagen, husband of Brünnhilde by treason.

Hagen (barit.) Son of dwarf Alberich and Grimhilde (seduced by the gold of the dwarf), half brother of Gunther and Gutrune.

Gutrune (sopr.) Daughter of Gilbich and Grimhilde, sister of Gunther, half sister of Hagen, wife of Siegfried by treason.

INTRODUCTION

I recently saw the movie *Troy* with Brad Pitt, directed by Wolfgang Peterson for Warner Bros. in 2004. I was really taken with this Hollywood production, inspired by Homer's *The Iliad*. I was so impressed by it that the minute I arrived home from the movie, I went to the library to search for my copy of *The Iliad*, which I had bought as a used book back in the seventies in Boston. It is nothing less than the translation of the book by Richmond Lattimore (1), considered to be one of the best, if not the best, translation in English of the famous Greek epic. Then, I started reading *The Iliad*: the gigantic poem of 15,693 verses, recounted in 24 books.

Of course, I had heard and been exposed to *The Iliad* since I was in elementary school in the sixth grade, when we studied the poem, and later my class undertook the representation of Homer's gigantic work (what a task for sixth graders!). It was a good job, though, just short episodes of the work! I vividly recall that Achilleus was played by the handsomest boy in the class, the one with whom we girls were in love. He was tall and showed a great body, dressed in the Greek tunic. I wonder where he is now.

During the first adult reading of *The Iliad*, I was now possessed by the book and could not put it down. I read the lengthy introduction by Mr. Lattimore and went on to read the poem written in dactylic hexameter. I could not get over the tremendous force describing the fights in the battles, whether it was Patroklos, Hektor, or Achilleus, how they slaughtered everything that crossed their paths; and how, not content with hitting their enemy with their spears, they even proceeded to pull them out, bringing along the bowels of the victim. Very bloody and gruesome indeed.

I was very impressed by the glorious addresses to the fighters in the book; some of the battles, enhanced by special effects, are shown in the movie.

Speaks Hektor:

> *Trojans, Lykians, Dardanians who fight at close quarters,*
> *be men now, dear friends, remember your furious valour*
> *along the hollow ships, since I have seen with my own eyes*
> *how by the hand of Zeus their bravest man's arrows were baffled.*
>   (Book 15. 486-489, p. 322)

> *So he spoke, and stirred the spirit and strength in each man.*
> *But Aias on the other side called to his companions:*
> *'Shame, you Argives; here is the time of decision, whether*
> *we die, or live on still and beat back ruin from our vessels.*
> *Do you expect, if our ships fall to helm-shining Hektor,*
> *you will walk each of you back dryshod to the land of your fathers?*
> *Do you not hear how Hektor is stirring up all his people,*
> *how he is raging to set fire to our ships? He is not*
> *inviting you to come to a dance. He invites you to battle.'*
>   (500-508. p. 322)

The bravest of all men are the heroes of *The Iliad*.

Reading along, I came to think more and more about Wagner and his *Ring of the Nibelung*, thinking of the classical Greek influence in it. It is not without cause that *The Iliad* led me to think about

The Ring. Wagner had a classical education in Germany and grew to be a lover of the Greeks, so that much of the thinking in *The Ring* came from the Greeks and the Greek tragedy and drama. Greek literature and the Greek philosophers fired Wagner's ideas exposed in his prose works, especially in *Art and Revolution*, written in 1849, as well as in *The Ring*.

Wagner also expounded his artistic ideas in his other prose works, *The Art Work of the Future* and *Opera and Drama*, both written during 1849-1852 while in exile in Zurich, where he took refuge after being forced to leave Germany due to his active participation in the Dresden uprising in 1849. During this same period, he wrote much of the text of *The Ring of the Nibelung*. During those years, he did not write a note of music but poured in prose what the theater and art of the future should be, based on his knowledge of Greek literature, tragedy, and drama. Later on, in 1860, he produced his work *The Music of the Future*, in which he makes considerations about the role of the orchestra in his dramas in relation to the chorus in the Greek tragedies.

As mentioned above, Wagner had had an extensive classical education in the German gymnasium, and at the age of thirteen, he had already translated twelve books of *The Odyssey* into German, to which he refers in his autobiography *My Life* (5). He had read the classical authors, Greek and Latin (he preferred the Greek), mythology, and ancient history. He wrote verses too and sketched out tragedies in the mood of the Greeks. All along his life, he and his wife, Cosima (Lizt's daughter), used to read after dinner quite often from *The Odyssey*; the works of the famous dramatists of the fifth century BC—Sophocles, Aeschylus, and Euripides—as well as Shakespeare, Cervantes, and others.

I would like to mention here two books, relatively new, which are devoted to what I have been writing here. One is by Jeffrey L.

Buller (*Classically Romantic: Classical Form and Meaning in Wagner's Ring*) (6); the other book is by Father M. Owen Lee (*Athena Sings: Wagner and the Greeks*) (8). The latter concentrates on the *Oresteia* of Aeschylus and his influence on Wagner. To quote from *Athena Sings*: "Surprisingly little has been written about the pervasive influence of classical Greece in the quintessentially German master" (8). These books, written with the Wagner enthusiast in mind, are very illustrative and easy to read. They have extensive notes and bibliography.

Buller brings out reference to some elements taken from Greek literature and incorporated by Wagner in *The Ring*. Let us mention, for instance, "the fights" between Wotan and his wife, Fricka, in *The Valkyrie* and those between Zeus (god of gods) and his wife (and sister as well), Hera, in *The Iliad*. I will refer to these later on. Such quarrels also occur between Odin and his wife, Frigga, in the Norse mythology, one of the main sources of *The Ring*.

The sources of *The Ring* were varied. Recent investigations have concluded that about 5 percent of *The Ring of the Nibelung* is derived from the Medieval thirteenth-century German epic *Das Nibelungenlied* (an epic second only to *The Iliad* in the history of Western literature) while 80 percent is from old Icelandic literature: the poetic and prose Eddas and the Volsunga saga (8), and other sources such as the German Thidreks sagas. All these works embody a literature of myths of diverse origins, which nurtured Wagner for his masterful creation of three operas, preceded by a prologue. These works are *The Rhinegold, The Valkyrie, Siegfried,* and *The Twilight of the Gods* (4).

I know the text of *The Ring* rather well, having seen the complete Tetralogy nine times: twice in Boston in the mideighties, one being the production of the Boston Lyric Opera conducted by John Balme; twice in the Metropolitan Opera in New York, which were productions of Otto Schenk (1997 and 2004) conducted by James Levine; three times in Bayreuth which included the 1995 production of Alfred Kirchner and Rosalie conducted by James Levine and the productions of Jurgen Flimm and Erich Wonder in 2001 and 2002, conducted by Giuseppe Sinopoli and Adam Fischer respectively; once at the Berlin Staatsoper Unter den Linden in Berlin, which was the Harry Kupfer production conducted by Daniel Barenboim in 2002; and, finally, *The Ring* in Cologne, Germany, production of Robert Carsen, conducted by Jeffrey Tate in 2004. In addition, I have seen several times some of the isolated operas. Then, going through *The Ring* was relatively easy for me; I have read the text several times and listened to records of the Tetralogy over and over again.

I knew *The Iliad* less well and had to read it thoroughly first. I went over it more than once, looking for situations in it that resembled those in *The Ring*. I started this account by stating that reading *The Iliad* led me to think about Wagner's *Ring*, so I will refer to some such elements, instances of resemblance that I have found between these two works. For *The Ring*, I will use the English Singing translation by Andrew Porter (2) and for *The Iliad* the already-mentioned Richmond Lattimore's work.

A Search for the Ring of the Nibelung in the Iliad

When considering the construction of *The Ring* in the music, Wagner uses the *leitmotifs*—that is, short fragments of music that identify characters, objects, states of mind, places, and other. We recognize the characters by their leitmotifs; and the music will sound in the orchestra when such objects, characters, places, etc., are being referred to, also, when they are being thought of by a character. As such, Wotan's spear and Siegmund's/Siegfried's sword have their leimotifs: the ring, the curse, the dragon, the giants, etc. They have been studied in detail by Deryck Cooke in his now-famous CD, *The Ring of the Nibelung*, and in *The Ring* disc (a CD-ROM, an interactive guide to Wagner's *Ring* cycle. 1999, Ring Disk Incorporated [http://www.ringdisc.net]).

In the style of *The Iliad*, we find that Homer uses single adjectives such as "huge," "fair headed," "glancing eyed," "deep girdled"; or adheres epithets such as "ox eyed," etc., to refer to his characters. Here are some cases taken from Lattimore's translation (1):

"Achilleus of the swift feet" (pp. 68, 206, 373, 377, 380, etc.);
Achilleus is often mentioned as just "Achilleus," or as "Peleus' son, Achilleus" (p. 59, first line of *The Iliad*). Surprisingly enough, Achilleus' tendon is never mentioned.
"Agamemnon, the lord of men" (pp. 120, 121, etc.);

"Agamemnon, son of Atreus" (pp. 69, 76, 81, 199, 304, etc.);

"Andromache of the white arms" (p. 163, etc.);

"Gray-eyed Athene, the lovely haired" (pp. 131, 139, 147, 151,
    155, 160, 161, 381, etc.);

"Helen of Argos" (pp. 113, 161, etc.);

"Hektor breaker of horses" (p. 404, the last line of The Iliad, and
    other places);

"Hektor of the bronze helm" (p.163, etc.);

"Hektor of the shining helm" (pp. 146, 160, 162, 167, 175, 192,
    etc.);

"Hera the goddess of the white arms" (pp. 60, 64, 75, 149, 301,
    etc.);

"Lord Zeus, the son of Kronos" (pp. 72, 73, 173, 186, 187,
    193, 198, 303, 378, etc);

"Swift-footed Achilleus" (pp. 214, 215, 280, 331, 452, etc.);

"Tall Hektor of the glancing helm" (pp. 97, 162, 165, 172, 174,
    176, etc.);

"The Gerenian horseman, Nestor" (pp. 85, 87, 92, 170, 172, 173,
    185, etc.);

"The ox-eyed lady Hera" (pp. 74, 75, 114, 194, 298, 301, 310,
    381, etc.);

"Zeus, the clouds gatherer" (pp. 74, 183, etc.);

"Zeus of the Aegis" (pp. 65, 80, 84, 85, 164, 180, etc.);

I would like to continue by referring to the elements of resemblance
that I have found between *The Ring of the Nibelung* and *The Iliad*.
The subtitle of this work, *A Search for The Ring of the Nibelung in
the Iliad*, may not be the most felicitous one. I recognize that the
elements, situations, moments, and instances in *The Ring* for which
I have found some echoing references in *The Iliad* do not occur in
a sequential order in the text of *The Iliad*. Nevertheless, I will let
the title stand. The elements of any similarity found do not appear
in linearity in *The Iliad*; they are rather "punctual" situations that
I have found all over the twenty-four books of *The Iliad*.

Table II

Chronology of *The Ring of the Nibelung* (3)

	Text	Music
The Rhinegold	1852	1853-1854
The Valkyrie	1852	1854
Siegfried	1851	1856-1857; 1869-1871
The Twilight of the Gods	1848-1852	1873-1874

Wagner stopped writing the music of *Siegfried* near the end of the second act. He then wrote *Tristan und Isolde*, text and music (1861-1867). He also wrote *Die Meistersingers* during this period. He came back to finish the second act of *Siegfried* in 1869, that is, after a hiatus of twelve years. Surprisingly enough, after such a long period away from *The Ring*, he was able to continue the music of *Siegfried* as if nothing had happened and maintained the line of the music and the unity of the work. The texts of the four operas were privately printed in 1853 under the title *The Ring of the Nibelung*. Once finished, the operas were performed separately prior to the **premiere** of the Tetralogy in 1876 in Bayreuth, in the theater the Festspielhaus (figure 5), which Wagner built to perform his operas exclusively.

SYNOPSIS

Books, books, books—many books have been written about psychological interpretations and philosophical implications and ideas embedded in Wagner's *Ring*, but we are not concerned with those matters here; we are concerned with the story as is, first reading.

The Rhinegold

Figure 1

The *Ring of the Nibelung* is a story of gods, goddesses, dwarves, giants, mortal men, vassals, and even a dragon. Usually, it is considered that there is a prologue (*Rhinegold*) and three operas in order (*The Valkyrie, Siegfried,* and *The Twilight of the Gods*). Then there is the story of a magic golden ring, forged by the dwarf Mime for his brother Alberich (king of the Nibelungs) who, in turn, stole the gold from the bottom of the river Rhine while the guardians, the Rhinemaidens, were distracted.

The god of gods, Wotan, needs to pay the giants Fasolt and Fafner for the building of his palace, Walhall. He does not have the money, so at first, he intends to pay them with the goddess Freia (goddess of love and youth), but the gods complain about it. It happens that he is helped by the god Loge (the god of fire) to steal Alberich's treasure, which includes the magic golden ring and the magic tarnhelm; then he will be able to pay the giants. Wotan, however, wishes to preserve the ring for himself, and at this point, Alberich curses the ring, which will cause the death of whoever possesses it. Wotan gives up the ring by the advice of the goddess of the earth, Erda; but he has already been touched by the cursed ring, and Erda announces to Wotan that the destruction of the gods is underway. Having paid the giants, Wotan and his wife, Fricka; the other gods and goddesses; and the Valkyries (Wotan's daughters from Erda) walk happily into Walhall. All the while, Wotan has been thinking of some independent agent who will recover the ring from the giant Fafner (now converted into a dragon who lives in a cave).

The Valkyrie

WOTAN

FRICKA

BRÜNNHILDE

HUNDING

SIEGLINDE AND SIEGMUND

Figure 2

Time has passed, and Wotan tries to use his son Siegmund (born from Erda) to recover the ring. In a stormy night, Siegmund, fleeing from his enemies, arrives at Sieglinde´s house, his twin sister, from whom he was separated years ago when they were children. She is unhappily married to Hunding who, after some discussion, allows Siegmund to stay overnight, but for sure, they will battle in the morning. Hunding is put to sleep under a potion given to him by Sieglinde. Left alone, the twins recognize each other and rapidly fall in love. Sieglinde tells Siegmund about the sword locked in the ash-tree inside the house by a strange guest who was present at her marriage. No one has been able to remove that sword from the tree. The strange guest was Wotan in disguise while on earth and known as Wälse; Siegmund proceeds to grasp the handle of the sword and, with a powerful effort, rapidly removes it from the tree; this is the magical sword, Notung, which his father had promised him. This is his gift to Sieglinde. He claims her as his bride, and they run out of the house into the moonlit spring night where they will consummate their love; Siegfried, of the opera *Siegfried*, will be their son.

Now Fricka, Wotan's wife and goddess of marriage, will convince him that he has helped Siegmund all along to recover the sword; and now Siegmund and Sieglinde, the incestuous pair, have wronged Hunding by running away together. She tells Wotan not to ask Brünnhilde, the Valkyrie and Wotan's favorite daughter, to help Siegmund. Wotan falls in despair and promises what Fricka asks. The battle takes place; and during it, Brünnhilde, disobeying Wotan, tries to help Siegmund. Wotan does make Hunding to strike Siegmund mortally, and he dies.

Now Wotan goes in pursuit of Brünnhilde, and his other eight daughters—Brünnhilde's sisters, the Valkyries—try to protect her. Brünnhilde rescues Sieglinde and the pieces of the broken Notung's sword and directs Sieglinde to rush into the forest, away from Wotan. The god punishes his daughter—she is put to sleep, a long sleep, on a rocky mountain surrounded by fire, as she had asked; only a hero without fear will be able to pass over the fire and rescue her. Wotan deprives Brünnhilde of her divinity, so that when she awakens, she will be a mortal woman.

Siegfried

SIEGFRIED KILLS THE DRAGON

THE WANDERER

BRÜNNHILDE

ALBERICH

ERDA

MIME

Figure 3

The hero, now a young boy, lives in the forest with the dwarf Mime, brother of Alberich. Mime helped Sieglinde during the birth of her son, when she died, and he has taken care of the boy ever since. Mime has not been able to forge the pieces of Notung for Siegfried, and finally Siegfried himself does it. He hates Mime and rapidly proceeds to kill the poor dwarf. Siegfried ventures into the woods where he finds the cave of the giant Fafner, converted into a dragon, now guarding the hoard of the gold. Siegfried, being fearless, kills the dragon and takes with him the golden ring and the magic tarnhelm, which makes invisible whoever wears it. Through understanding the song of a bird, which follows him (an emissary of Wotan), he finds out about the maiden sleeping on a rock surrounded by fire. There he goes, again being fearless; he crosses the fire, awakens Brünnhilde, falls in love with her, and they marry. He gives Brünnhilde the ring as a token of love, and she gives him her horse, Grane. Following Brünnhilde's desires, he ventures into the world in search of adventures.

The Twilight of the Gods

SIEGFRIED

GUNTHER

GUTRUNE

Figure 4a

ALBERICH

HAGEN

BRÜNNHILDE

WALTRAUTE

Figure 4b

Presently, Siegfried arrives into the kingdom of the Gibichungs whose king is Gunther, half brother of Gutrune and Hagen, the latter being the son of Alberich. Siegfried and Gunther sign a pact of blood by which Siegfried is to marry Gutrune, and he will offer Brünnhilde to Gunther. When they sign the pact, Siegfried was under the effect of a potion given him by Gutrune that made him forget that he was already married to the Valkyrie. Siegfried and Gunther soon depart to bring Brünnhilde to the palace. Siegfried is carrying the magic tarnhelm, which makes him invisible, when he comes to Brünhilde's cave. The Valkyrie offers some resistance to the invader but to no avail; Siegfried takes the ring from her hand and abducts her from the cave. Upon arrival to the Gibichungs' hall, everything is ready for the wedding of Siegfried and Gutrune. Brünnhilde notices the ring in Siegfried's hand, and she knows he was her abductor who plans to marry Gutrune.

She screams, "Treason, the traitor should die!" But how? Hagen
is willing to arrange a hunting trip during which the hero will be
killed. During the hunt, he gives Siegfried a potion, and he now
remembers that Brünnhilde is his wife. Hagen strikes him in the
back, the only place where the hero is vulnerable, and he dies.
Siegfried's body is brought to the Gibichungs' hall. Hagen has been
trying to get hold of the ring all along; he reaches to Siegfried to
remove the ring, but then the hero lifts his menacing hand, and
Hagen retreats. Brünnhilde orders to lit a pyre for Siegfried's body
to be burned and, assessing the situation, decides to immolate
herself and her horse together with her lover. The pyre is lit, and
before jumping into it, she hurls an ignited branch into Walhall
where Wotan—sitting with his gods and goddesses, valkyries, and
heroes—is consumed by the fire. The river Rhine overflows and in
time will put the fire of the pyre out. Hagen asks the Rhinemaidens
to give him the ring; but they throw it back into the swollen river,
then hold Hagen by the back, and drown him. The entire world
is consumed by fire. A new world will come to be.

1

Dwelling of the Gods

a. *Mists and clouds.* The dwelling of the gods. I will start by considering the beginning of *Rhinegold*, prologue to the scenic festival that is *The Ring of the Nibelung*. In it, there are mists and clouds, which abound in *The Ring*. In scene 1, describing the stage, Wagner writes, "Towards the bottom [of the stage], the waters [of the river Rhine] resolve into an increasingly fine damp mist, so that a space a man's height from the ground seems to be completely free of the water, which courses like a train of clouds over the dusky bed." (*Rhinegold*, scene 1, p. 3). In scene 2, "The waves are gradually transformed into clouds" and later "resolving to fine mist." Later on, in an open space on a mountaintop, a castle appears. This is Walhall, the dwelling of the gods. (*Rhinegold*, scene 2, p. 18).

And in scene 4, Wotan, the god of gods, turns solemnly to his wife, Fricka:

Wotan:

> *So greet I the hall,*
> *safe from all fear and dread.*
> *Follow me, wife:*
> *in Walhall, reign there with me!*

> (*Rhinegold*, scene 4, p. 70)

Mime in *Siegfried*:

> *Much, Wanderer,*
> *much you know*
> *of the earth and all her dwellers.*
> *But can now you say*
> *what lordly race*
> *dwells on cloud-hidden heights?*

Wanderer (Wotan's name when on earth):

> *On cloud-hidden heights—*
> *that's where the gods dwell;*
> *Walhall is their home.*
>
> *(Siegfried,* act 1, scene 2, p. 172)

In *The Iliad*, Zeus, the gatherer of the clouds, lives in Olympos:

> *Now Dawn the yellow-robed scattered over all the earth. Zeus*
> *who joys in the thunder made an assembly of all the immortals*
> *upon the highest peak of rugged Olympos. There he*
> *spoke to them himself, and the other divinities listened:*
> *'Hear me, all of you gods and all you goddesses: Hear me*
> *while I speak forth what the heart within my breast urges.'*
>
> (8. 1-6, p. 182)

Zeus is often referred to as the cloud gatherer, and Olympos as "rugged in the tall sky," from which I gather that mists and clouds are not strange elements in Olympos.

Zeus, as gatherer of clouds, talking to the goddess Athena:

> *Then Zeus the gatherer of the clouds smiled at her and answered:*

'Tritogeneia, dear daughter, do not lose heart; for I say this
not in outright anger, and my meaning toward you is kindly.'
(8. 38-40, p. 183)

Thetis, Zeus' daughter, talking to her father when she goes to supplicate him in favor of her son Achilleus:

She spoke thus. But Zeus who gathers the clouds, made no answer
but sat in silence a long time. And Thetis, as she had taken
his knees, clung fast to them and urged once more her question:
'Bend your head and promise me to accomplish this thing.'
(1. 511-514, p.72)

Deeply disturbed Zeus who gathers the clouds answered her:
'This is a disastrous matter when you set me in conflict
with Hera, and she troubles me with recriminations.'
(517-519, p. 73)

b. *Lightning and thunder.* In *Rhinegold*, there is a god of lightning and thunder, Donner, who gathers the clouds.

Donner:

Sweltering mists
hang in the air;
I'm oppressed
by their gloomy weight.
I'll gather the clouds,
summon the lightning and thunder
to sweep the mist from the sky!
(*Rhinegold*, scene 4, p. 69)

The stage directions read, "He climbs onto a high rock by the precipice and there swings his hammer. Mists gather around him" (*Rhinegold*, scene 4, p. 69). Later on in the same scene, "his hammer-blow is heard striking hard on the rock". He summons his brother Froh:

> *Brother, to me!*
> *Show them the bridge to the hall.*
>
> (p. 69)

The gods will ascend the bridge to reach Walhall, up in the clouds. "While the gods are crossing the bridge to the castle, the curtain falls in *Rhinegold*" (*Rhinegold*, scene 4, p. 72).

In *The Iliad*:

Thetis talks to Achilleus when she promised him to go to Zeus and intercede in his favor:

> *But I will go to cloud-dark Olympos and ask this*
> *thing of Zeus who delights in the thunder. Perhaps he will do it.*
>
> (1. 419-420, p. 70)

Hephaistos consoling his mother Hera after Zeus has had an argument with her:

> *Hephaistos the renowned smith rose up to speak among them,*
> *to bring comfort to his beloved mother, Hera of the white arms:*
> *'This will be a disastrous matter and not endurable*
> *if you two are to quarrel thus for the sake of mortals*
> *and bring brawling among the gods. There will be no pleasure*
> *in the stately feast at all, since the vile things will be uppermost.*
> *And I entreat my mother, though she herself understands it,*
> *to be ingratiating toward our father Zeus, that no longer*

our father may scold her and break up the quiet of our feasting.
For if the Olympian who handles the lightning should be minded
to hurl us out of our places, he's far too strong for any.'

(571-581, p. 74)

Zeus the Olympian and lord of the lightning went to
his own bed, where always he lay when sweet sleep came on him.
Going up to the bed he slept and Hera of the gold throne beside him.

(609-611, p. 75)

2

The Company of the Gods

Wotan lives in Walhall with all the gods and goddesses; his daughters, the Valkyries; and the dead heroes collected in the battlefields by the Valkyries.

Siegmund when Brünnhilde invites him to Walhall:

> *Then greet for me Walhall,*
> *greet for me Wotan,*
>
> *and all the heroes;*
> *greet all those fair*
> *and lovely maidens.*
> *To Walhall I will not go!*
>
> (*Valkyrie*, act 2, scene 4, pp. 118-119)

In *The Iliad*, Zeus lives in Olympos with all the gods and goddesses, and the muses, who are nine; and they are the inspirers of the artists and the scientists:

> *Tell me now, you Muses who have your homes on Olympos.*
> *For you, who are goddesses, are there, and you know all things,*
> *and we have heard only the rumor of it and know nothing.*
>
> (2. 484-486, p. 89)

. . . . For no longer are the gods who live in Olympos
arguing the matter, since Hera has forced them all over
by her supplication, and evils are in store for the Trojans
by Zeus' will.

(67-70, p. 78)

But when the twelfth dawn after this day appeared, the gods who
live forever came back to Olympos all in a body
and Zeus led them;

(1. 493-495, p. 72)

3

Wotan Carries an Ash Spear; So Do Hunding, Brünnhilde, Hagen, and Others

The spear is Wotan's emblem of power, where his contracts and treaties are carved. When he cut the branch of the sacred ash-tree, he committed his first sin, his original sin against nature. He made the spear with such branch; the spear is an instrument of war, but it is not used for war by Wotan. In it, he has carved all the treaties, contracts, and bargains; and he uses it as the symbol of his power.

The first Norn, one of Erda's daughters, sings:

> *From the World Ash-tree*
> *mighty Wotan broke a branch;*
> *and his spear was shaped*
> *from that branch he tore from the tree.*
> (*Twilight of the Gods*, prelude, p. 248)

The wanderer, Wotan, also tells the story of the ash spear:

> *From the world-ashtree's*
> *sacred branches*
> *Wotan once tore his spear:*

> *dead the tree—*
> *but still mighty the spear;*
> *and with that spear point*
> *Wotan rules the world.*
> *Bargains and contracts,*
> *bonds and treaties,*
> *deep in that shaft he graved.*
> *Who holds that spear-shaft*
> *rules the world;*
>
> (*Siegfried*, act 1, scene 2, pp. 172-173)

In *The Iliad*, I did not find any reference to Zeus using an ash spear, but the heroes and the fighting men do have ash spears, which often have the heads covered with bronze.

King Agamemnon:

> . . . . *Menelaos shoved with his hand Adrestos*
> *the warrior back from him, and powerful Agamemnon*
> *stabbed him in the side and, as he writhed over, Atreides,*
> *setting his heel upon the midriff, wrenched out the ash spear.*
>
> (6. 62-65, pp. 154-155)

Diomedes fighting against Ares, god of war:

> *After him Diomedes of the great war cry drove forward*
> *with the bronze spear; and Pallas Athene, leaning in on it,*
> *drove it into the depth of the belly where the war belt girt him.*
> *Picking this place she stabbed and driving it deep in the fair flesh*
> *wrenched the spear out again.*
>
> (5. 855-859, p. 151)

King Priam of Troy, Hektor's father, also carries an ash spear.

Hektor speaking:

> *For I know this thing well in my heart, and my mind knows it:*
> *there will come a day when sacred Ilion shall perish,*
> *and Priam, and the people of Priam of the strong ash spear.*
>
> (6. 447-449. p. 165)

These two lines are repeated at least in these two instances: (4. 164, p. 117) and (8. 551, p. 197),

Hektor's ash spear:

> *While Hektor with the sharp spear struck Eioneus, under*
> *the circle of the bronze helm, in the neck, and broke his limbs' strength.*
>
> (7. 11-12, p. 168)

> *Hektor stood up close to Aias and hacked at the ash spear*
> *with his great sword, striking behind the socket of the spearhead,*
> *and slashed it clean away, so that Telamonian Aias*
> *shook there in his hand a lopped spear, while far away from him*
> *the bronze spearhead fell echoing to the ground;*
>
> (16. 114-118, p. 333)

Alexandros (Paris) fighting Menelaos:

> *First of the two Alexandros let go his spear far-shadowing*
> *and struck the shield of Atreus' son on its perfect circle*
> *nor did the bronze point break its way through, but the spearhead bent*
>   *back*
> *in the strong shield.*
>
> (1. 346-359, p. 109)

Achilleus:

> *There standing the goddess of the white arms, Hera, shouted,*
>
> *'Shame, you Argives, poor nonentities splendid to look on.*
> *In those days when brilliant Achilleus came into the fighting,*
> *never would the Trojans venture beyond the Dardanian*
> *gates, so much did they dread the heavy spear of that man.*
> *Now they fight by the hollow ships and far from the city.'*
>
> (5. 784, 787-791, p. 149)

Patroklos, getting ready for battle, arms himself with Achilleus's ash spear:

> *He took up two powerful spears that fitted his hand's grip,*
> *only he did not take the spear of blameless Aiakides,*
> *huge, heavy, thick, which no one else of all the Achaians*
> *could handle, but Achilleus alone knew how to wield it;*
> *the Pelian ash spear which Cheiron had brought to his father*
> *from high on Pelion to be death for fighters.*
>
> (16. 139-144, p. 334)

4

Walhall

Walhall is the abode of the gods. It first appears in the second scene of *The Rhinegold*; as do Wotan and his wife, Fricka. They are sleeping in a "flowery bed" at the side of the river Rhine. Fricka awakes and sees the castle on top of the mountain; then she calls her husband.

Fricka:

> *Wotan, my lord! awaken!*

Wotan:

> *The sacred hall of the gods*
> *is guarded by gate and door:*
> > *manhood's honour,*
> > *unending power,*
> *rise now to endless renown!*

(Rhinegold, scene 2, pp. 18, 19)

Wotan:

> *Completed, the eternal work !*
> > *On mountain summits*
> > *the gods will rule!*
> > *Proudly rise*
> > *those glittering walls*

which in dreams I designed,
which my will brought to life.
  Strong and lordly
  see it shine;
holy, glorious abode!

(p. 19)

Wotan has contracted two members of the race of the giants—who lived in Riesenheim, the giants Fafner and Fasolt—to construct the castle and has promised them as payment the goddess Freia. She grows the golden apples that the gods eat to preserve their youth.

Fricka:

  Though it delights you,
  I am afraid!
  You have your hall,
  but I think of Freia!
  Can I believe you have forgotten
  the price you still have to pay?
    The work is finished,
    the giants must be paid;
  remember it, all that you owe!

Wotan:

  I've not forgotten the bargain,
  the giants shall have their reward;

(p. 19)

Fricka:

  If I had known of your deal,
  I might have stopped it in time;

> *but slyly you men*
>   *did your talking in secret,*
> *and kept us women away;*
> *alone you discussed with the giants.*
>
> *Nothing is sacred,*
>   *you harden your hearts,*
> *when you men lust for might!*

(p. 20)

Wotan does not really intend to pay the giants with Freia, but will call for the god Loge to help him.

Freia:

> *Help me, sister!*
> *shelter me, brother!*
> *On yonder mountain*
> *Fasolt is threatening,*
> *and now he's coming to take me.*

(p. 21)

In *The Iliad*, there is a situation that resembles the construction of Walhall by the giants, as follows.

Poseidon to Apollo Phoibos:

> *. . . . Can you not even*
> *now remember all the evils we endured here by Ilion,*
> *you and I alone of the gods, when to proud Laomedon*
> *we came down from Zeus and for a year were his servants*
> *for a stated hire, and he told us what to do, and to do it?*
> *Then I built a wall for the Trojans about their city,*
> *wide, and very splendid, so none could break into their city,*

but you, Phoibos, herded his shambling horn-curved cattle
along the spurs of Ida with all her folds and her forests.
But when the changing seasons brought on the time for our labour
to be paid, then headstrong Laomedon violated and made void
all our hire, and sent us away, and sent threats after us.
For he threatened to hobble our feet and to bind our arms,
to carry us away for slaves in the far-lying islands.
He was even going to strip with bronze the ears from both of us.

(21. 441-455, p. 430)

Buller (6) relates an outcome to this story, but strangely, I did not find it in the translation of *The Iliad* with which I am working. His narration says that the gods decided to punish the Trojan king and sent a sea monster, which would have threatened the destruction of Ilion unless the king allowed the monster to devour his daughter Hesione. There appeared Heracles who offered to kill the monster if he could get Hesione in return. Once this was done, the king still persisted with his general negative attitude. This story in *The Iliad* then reminds the construction of Walhall by the giants, and Wotan refuses to pay them with the goddess Freia as initially promised.

5

God of Fire, Loge

The god of fire in *The Ring* is Loge. Wotan summons Loge when he needs him to solve problems as in *Rhinegold*, scene 2. Wotan has made a deal with the giants, Fasolt and Fafner, to pay them with the goddess Freia, goddess of fertility and youth and the sister of Fricka, for the construction of the castle Walhall.

Fricka and her brothers, Donner and Froh, protest strongly. The giants come to ask for their prize, and Wotan wishes to get off the deal; but the giants are not ready to back the promise and take Freia with them. Wotan calls Loge, the god of fire, to help him solve the situation. Loge does arrive; and after much scheming, he tells Wotan that the solution is to steal the gold and the magic tarnhelm and the ring from the Nibelung Alberich—who, in turn, stole it from the river Rhine—and give it to the giants, who, after all, care more about gold than about the goddess of love, Freia.

Loge and Wotan embark to Nibelheim in scene 3 of *Rhinegold*, steal the gold, not without trouble, return, and pay the giants in scene 4; and then Freia is liberated.

Loge tells Wotan:

> *A magic spell*
> *can change the gold to a ring.*
> *No one knows it,*

but he who would use the spell
must curse the joys of love.

(*Rhinegold*, scene 2, p. 31)

When Wotan asks how to get the gold from Alberich, Loge answers him:

By theft!
What a thief stole,
  you steal from the thief;
you seize it and make it your own!

(p. 32)

Fafner, one of the giants:

Hear, Wotan,
  I'll speak my last word!
We will leave you with Freia;
  we will take less
    for our payment:
for us rude giants, enough
is Nibelheim's shining gold.

(p. 33)

Wotan:

Come, Loge,
  descend with me!
To Nibelheim we'll go together:
and there I'll win me the gold.

(p. 36)

Once in Niebelheim, Wotan and Loge force Alberich to give them the hoard of gold, the tarnhelm, and the ring. Alberich does not want to yield the ring, and when the ring is finally removed from his finger, he curses it.

Alberich:

> *Am I now free?*
> *truly free?*
> *I greet you then*
> *in my freedom: mark my words!*
> *Since a curse gained it for me,*
> *my curse lies on this ring!*
> *   Though its gold*
> *   brought riches to me,*
> *   let now it bring*
> *but death, death to its lord!*

(scene 4, p. 58)

Once Freia is free and the gold has been paid to the giants, the gods will ascend the bridge to Walhall at the end of *Rhinegold*.

Wotan will call Loge again at the end of the third act of *The Valkyrie* to order him to kindle the fire around the rock where he has put Brünnhilde to sleep. Loge appears this time not as a character but as a flame that ignites the fire around the rock, and Wotan will spread it with his spear to form a circle around the rock.

In *The Iliad*, the god of fire is Hephaistos. Achilleus has been fighting against the Trojans by the side of the river Xanthios and has killed many men and thrown them with the heavy armor inside the river. Then the river became furious and turned into a big wave that terrified Achilleus and made him run for safety, but the strength of the water in high waves was about to overrun the hero.

Apollo and Athene appeared and tried to help Achilleus, but it was not until Hera called Hephaistos—her son, god of fire—that Achilleus was safe. Hephaistos turned ablaze all over and around the river:

> *Hera spoke, and Hephaistos set on them an inhuman fire.*
> *First he kindled a fire in the plain and burned the numerous*
> *corpses that lay there in abundance, slain by Achilleus,*
> *and all the plain was parched and the shining water was straitened.*
> (21. 342-345, p. 427)

The river called Hephaistos and asked him to call off the fire:

> . . . . *'Hephaistos, not one of the gods could stand up against you.*
> *I for one could not fight the flame of a fire like this one.*
> *Leave your attack. Brilliant Achilleus can capture the city*
> *of the Trojans, now, for me. What have I to do with this quarrel?'*
> (357-360, p. 427)

> *Now when the goddess of the white arms, Hera, had heard this*
> *immediately she spoke to her own dear son, Hephaistos:*
> *'Hephaistos, hold, my glorious child, since it is not fitting*
> *to batter thus an immortal god for the sake of mortals.'*
> *So she spoke, and Hephaistos quenched his inhuman fire. Now*
> *the lovely waters ran their ripples back in the channel.*
> (377-382, p. 428)

6

Goddess of Earth, Erda

In *The Ring*. Wagner's stage directions: the stage is dark, "a bluish light breaks from the rocky cleft at the side, and in it Erda suddenly appears, rising from below to half her height. Her noble features are ringed by a mass of black hair" (*Rhinegold*, scene 4, p. 65). Nowadays, Erda may appear in all her stature down to her feet. The creative processes of the new productions may ignore Wagner's instructions, and sometimes the operas may become unrecognizable.

Erda appears in *Rhinegold* when all the gods are urging Wotan to give the golden ring to the giants to complete the payment of the castle.

Erda:

> *Yield it, Wotan, yield it!*
> *Yield the accursed ring!*
>   *Wretchedness,*
>   *doom and disaster*
> *lie there in the ring.*
>
> *All of the past, know I.*
>   *All things that are,*
>   *all things that shall be—*
>   *all I know:*

the endless world's
all wise one,
Erda, bids you beware.

Hear me! Hear me! Hear me!
All things that are, perish!
An evil day
dawns for the immortals:
I warn you, yield up the ring!
(Erda sinks slowly to breast level, as the bluish
glow begins to fade.)

(*Rhinegold*, scene 4, p. 65)

Wotan calls Erda in the third act, scene 1 of *Siegfried*. He is in
need of wisdom:

Erda! Erda!
Woman all-wise!
Waken, awaken,
O Wala! Awaken!

(*Siegfried*, act 3, scene 1, p. 221)

She is awakened by Wotan; but she cannot help him this time,
and she disappears. And Wotan says:

Return! Return
to endless sleep!

(act 1, scene 2, p. 225)

Wotan has been long awaiting for the end since the second act of
The Valkyrie when he confides with anguish to Brünnhilde. Wotan
continues walking his way through the forest and soon encounters
Siegfried. The young recognizes that he was the one responsible for
the death of his father, Siegmund, and he asks Wotan to let him

pass. Wotan holds his spear across him; and Siegfried, with a blow of his sword, breaks it into two pieces, which fall to the ground.

Wanderer (this is Wotan's name while he's on earth, in *Siegfried*):

> *Whatever may happen,*
> *the god will gladly*
> *yield his rule to the young!*
>
> (Siegfried, act 3, scene 2, p. 225)

> *Pass on! I cannot prevent you!*
>
> (p. 231)

This is the moment in *The Ring* when the god of gods is defeated, and the new man is emerging. This is the last time we see Wotan in *The Ring*, but we will hear about him again later on when Waltraute comes to visit Brünnhilde in her cave in *Twilight of the Gods* (act 1, scene 3, pp. 271-277).

In *The Iliad*, Achilleus talks to his mother, complaining about Agamemnon who has dishonored him. Thetis, emerging from the gray water, reminds Erda:

> *So he spoke in tears and the lady his mother heard him*
> *as she sat in the depths of the sea at the side of her aged father,*
> *and lightly she emerged like a mist from the grey water.*
> *She came and sat beside him as he wept, and stroked him*
> *with her hand and called him by name and spoke to him: 'Why then,*
> *child, do you lament? What sorrow has come to your heart now?*
> *Tell me, do not hide it in your mind, and thus we shall both know.'*
>
> (1. 357-363, p. 68)

7

Incest

In *The Ring*, incest occurs in the opera *The Valkyrie*, in the first act, where the incestuous pair, the twins Siegmund and Sieglinde, meets for the first time. They are Wotan's children who meet as adults after having been separated in childhood. Siegmund arrives at Sieglinde's house in a night of storm and tells his story:

Siegmund:

> *Ill-fate pursues me,*
> *follows my footsteps;*
>
> *This ill-fate you must not share!*
> *So I must leave your house.*

Sieglinde:

> *No, do not leave!*
> *You bring no ill fate to me,*
> *for ill fate has long been here!*
> (*The Valkyrie*, act 1, scene 1, pp. 78-79)

Hunding, her husband, arrives and challenges Siegmund to fight
on the next day:

> *For the night you are my guest.*
>   *But find some weapons*
>   *to serve you tomorrow;*
>
>   (scene 2, p. 85)

Siegmund is left alone and pleads to his father for the sword he
has promised him in the moment of need:

> *A sword was pledged by my father,*
> *to serve in my hour of need.*
>   *I am unarmed*
>   *in my enemy's house;*
>
>   (scene 3, p. 86)

Sieglinde comes to join him, and looking sternly at each other's
faces, they begin to recognize themselves as brother and sister and
fall in love. Later, with a powerful effort, so described by Wagner,
Siegmund removes the sword, Notung, from the ash-tree to where
Sieglinde has pointed out.

Elated, Siegmund sings:

> *Siegmund, the Wälsung,*
> *here you see!*
> *As bride—gift*
> *he brings you this sword;*
> *he claims with it*
> *his loveliest bride;*
> *and from this house*
> *he leads her away.*

> *Bride and sister*
> *be to your brother;*
> *the blood of these Wälsungs is blessed!*
>   (*Valkyrie*, act 1, scene 3, pp. 94-95)

And they run out into the spring moonlit night. Siegfried will be the product of their union.

Wagner brings incest into *The Ring* possibly as a means to purify the race, to ensure that the progeny of the twins will be the kind of hero who, without divine guidance, will take the mission to serve Wotan's designs. Incest in some cultures of antiquity—Egypt, among the Incas—was used to ensure the preservation of the royal lineage.

In *The Iliad*, the incestuous pair is Zeus and Hera; they are brother and sister. The word "incest" is mentioned nowhere in *The Iliad*. They live in Olympos, somehow happily in the company of the other gods and goddesses and the muses. At times, Zeus is harsh to Hera in the manner of Wotan to Fricka, and Wagner himself to his wife, Minna.

Zeus speaks:

> *'Hera, do not go on hoping that you will hear all my*
> *thoughts, since these will be too hard for you, though you are my wife.*
> *Any thought that it is right for you to listen to, no one*
> *neither man nor any immortal shall hear it before you.*
> *But anything that apart from the rest of the gods I wish to*
> *plan, do not always question each detail nor probe me.'*
>   (1. 545-550, p. 73)

8

Potions

Potions are often prepared in *The Ring* for the benefit of one character to obtain a desired effect and to the detriment of another character. Those instances are listed below:

a. Sieglinde prepares a potion for Hunding

Sieglinde:

Are you awake?

Siegmund:

Who steals this way?

Sieglinde:

I do. Listen to me!
In heavy sleep lies Hunding;
I gave him a drug in his drink.
Now, in the night, you are safe!

Siegmund:

Safe when you are near!

Sieglinde:

There's a sword for him who can win it;
and when that sword is won,
*   then I can call you*
*   noblest of heroes:*
*   the strongest alone*
*   masters the sword.*

(*Valkyrie*, act 1, scene 3, pp. 87-88)

b. In the opera *Siegfried*, Mime is brewing a concoction of herbs, with which he plans to kill his adopted son Siegfried.

Mime:

He's forging a bright, sharp sword.
*   Fafner will feel it*
*   and meet his death.*
I've brewed a deadly drink;
*   Siegfried will follow*
*   when Fafner's dead.*
My skill will gain me the prize;
ring and gold will be mine!

(*Siegfried*, act 1, scene 3, p. 187)

Siegfried forges the sword; goes into the forest and kills the dragon, Fafner, who was guarding Alberich's pile of gold; and removes the tarnhelm and the gold ring. Then he sits down. Mime is nearby, hoping for the opportunity to make Siegfried drink his potion. Then he steals the tarnhelm and the ring from him.

Mime:

> *Now, my Wälsung!*
> *Wolf's son you!*
> *Drink and choke to death!*
> *You'll never drink again!*

(act 2, scene 3, p. 216)

Siegfried lifts his sword and aims at Mime, who falls dead immediately.

c. Siegfried arrives at the Gibichung's kingdom. Gutrune, Gunther's sister, prepares a potion that when drunk by Siegfried makes him totally forget his past. Siegfried learns that Gunther is single; then he offers to bring Brünnhilde to him as a wife so that he can marry Gutrune.

Gunther:

> *Gutrun I'll give to you gladly.*

Siegfried:

> *Brünnhilde then is yours.*

Gunther:

> *But how will you deceive her?*

Siegfried:

> *By the Tarnhelm's art*
> *I can be changed into you.*

Gunther:

> *Then let us swear by a vow!*

Siegfried:

> *Blood brotherhood*
> *joins us as one!*

They proceed to the ritual. Hagen pours wine into a horn, and Siegfried and Gunther cut their arms with their swords and let the blood drop into the horn.

Both:

> *Truth I swear to my friend!*
> *Fair and free,*
> *the blood is our bond;*
> *blood—brotherhood here!*

Gunther:

> *If one friend should be false—*

Siegfried:

> *If one friend should betray—*

Both:

> *then not drops of blood—*
> *all his life blood*
> *shall flow in streams from his veins;*
> *traitors so must atone!*

Gunther (drinks):

> *I swear to be true!*

Siegfried:

> *I swear to be true!*

Siegfried also drinks.

Hagen does not join them in the blood brotherhood oath. Gunther and Siegfried leave by boat to reach Brünnhilde's cave.

> (*Twilight of the Gods*, act 1, scene 2, pp. 267-268)

d. Siegfried has betrayed Brünnhilde by abducting her from the cave and offering her as a wife to Gunther.

Brünnhilde (holding the point of her spear):

> *Shining steel!*
> *Holiest weapon!*
> *Help me defend my honour!*
>
> *Devote your mighty strength*
> *to his destruction!*
> *For his treachery he must die,*

strike him and kill him!
For he has betrayed every vow,
and falsehood now he has sworn!

(act 2, scene 4, p. 298)

Hagen offers to revenge her. He hopes to get the ring from Siegfried. A hunting trip will be arranged during which Hagen will kill the hero. Gutrune will be told that a wild boar has attacked and killed Siegfried. Siegfried is offered drinks more than once during a hunting trip, and he starts talking about himself and his past. Soon Hagen offers him a drinking horn into which he squeezes the juice of an herb.

Hagen:

Drink first, hero,
from my horn.
I have here a noble drink;
let its freshening power wake your
                                          remembrance
so none of the past escapes you.

Siegfried drinks from the horn and continues his tale of how he came to Brünnhilde's rock guided by the bird.

Siegfried:

Till I came to that fiery peak.
I passed through those dangers;
I found the maid . . .
sleeping . . . my glorious bride!
In shining armour she lay.
The helmet
I took from her head;

my kiss awakened the bride.
Oh, then like burning fire
I was held by lovely Brünnhilde's arms!

Hagen cries:

Vengeance!

Hagen furiously plunges his spear into Siegfried's back, the only area where the hero was vulnerable. Siegfried falls dead backward on his shield.

Gunther:

Hagen, you murdered him!

Hagen:

Falsehood is punished.

(act 3, scene 2, pp. 318-319)

Back at the palace, Hagen will give the news to Gutrune.

Hagen:

A ferocious boar has slain him;
Siegfried, your husband, is dead.

Gutrune:

Siegfried! Siegfried is murdered!

(p. 322)

She rejects Gunther, who is coming close to her, and blames him for the murder of her husband.

Gunther:

Cast not the blame on me,
but cast the blame on Hagen.
He is the boar who killed him;
by Hagen's spear he was slain.

(p. 323)

Brünnhilde:

Poor creature, peace!
For you and he were not wed;
his mistress,
but never his wife!
But I was his own true wife;
eternal devotion he'd sworn,
and Siegfried and Brünnhild were one!

Gutrune:

Accursed Hagen!
By your advice I gave him
the drink that made him forget!
Ah, sorrow!
My eyes are opened.
Brünnhild was his true love,
whom through the drink he forgot!

(pp. 324-325)

Brünnhilde orders the pyre to be set for Siegfried's funeral and decides to immolate herself next to her lover, together with her horse Grane and the ring. She will mount her horse and jump into the fire. She wishes to cleanse the world from all its vices, and the destruction that follows reaches Walhall and causes the end of the gods, as Erda had predicted in *Rhinegold*:

Hear me! Hear me! Hear me!
All things that are, perish!
  An evil day
  dawns for the immortals:
I warn you, yield up the ring!

(Rhinegold, scene 4, p. 65)

A new world will come to be.

(Twilight of the Gods, act 1, scene 3, pp 322-328)

In *The Iliad,* disaster! I did not find any instances of potions being prepared to be given to another person for his detriment. But I could not let pass the narrations of the potions that occur in *The Ring.* I will content myself here with saying that both the Greeks and the Trojans were given to dinners during which they consumed large amounts of meats from different animals cooked in huge bronze cauldrons or in barbecue fashion. They also consumed all along large quantities of wine; and afterward, everybody was happy, and they went to sleep. Nobody had been either tricked or hurt.

9

The Friction between Wotan and Fricka

I will refer to the long encounter between Wotan and Fricka in act 2, scene 1 of *The Valkyrie*, pp. 98-104.

Fricka is asking Wotan to punish the incestuous pair of Siegmund and his sister Sieglinde (Wotan's children), who have wronged Sieglinde's husband Hunding.

Fricka:

> *I have heard Hunding's cry:*
> *Revenge the wrong they have done!*
> > *As wedlock's guardian*
> > *I answered him.*
> > *I swore*
> > *I would punish the deed*
> *this pair dared to commit,*
> *who wronged a husband and me.*

(p. 98)

Wotan:

> *But what evil*
> > *have they done?*

The Spring enticed them to love.
The power of love
overcame them both;
and who can resist that power?

Fricka:

Pretend that you don't understand!
And yet you know all too well;
that I have come
to avenge marriage vows,
the holy vows they have broken!

Wotan:

Unholy
call I the vows
that bind unloving hearts;

(p. 98)

Fricka:

So this is the end
of the gods and their glory.

(p. 99)

Oh, why mourn
over virtue and vows,
when they first were broken by you!
Your faithful wife
you've always betrayed;

(p. 100)

Go on with your work!
Fill now my cup!
You betrayed me; let me be trampled!

(p. 100)

Wotan (quietly):

Your concern
is for things that have been;
but what is still to come—
to that turn all my thoughts.

(*Valkyrie*, act 2, scene 1, p. 100)

Fricka appears to be growing upset while Wotan is on the quiet side, though firm; and at the end, he will come out totally dejected and helpless. He has to surrender to Fricka and order his daughter Brünnhilde not to help Siegmund in the coming battle with Hunding. There, Siegmund perishes, much to Wotan's sadness.

Now in *The Iliad*, friction between Zeus and Hera:

Then the father of gods and men seeing Hektor pitied him
and looked scowling terribly at Hera, and spoke a word to her:
'Hopeless one, it was your evil design, your treachery, Hera,
that stayed brilliant Hektor from battle, terrified his people.
I do not know, perhaps for this contrivance of evil
and pain you will win first reward when I lash you with whip strokes.
Do you not remember that time you hung from high and on your feet
I slung two anvils, and about your hands drove a golden
chain, unbreakable. You among the clouds and the bright sky
hung, nor could the gods about tall Olympos endure it
and stood about, but could not set you free.

(15. 12-22, p. 309)

It appears that Zeus behaved as a brute to Hera who, of course, was frightened and claimed that the loss of fortune by Hektor and the Trojans was due to the god Poseidon, not to her.

In another occasion, Zeus is in a better mood:

> *'Hera, there will be a time afterwards when you can go there*
> *as well. But now let us go to bed and turn to love-making.*
> *For never before has love for any goddess or woman*
> *so melted about the heart inside me, broken it to submission,*
> *as now: not that time when I loved the wife of Ixion . . . .'*
>
> (14. 313-317, p. 302)

And he proceeds to enumerate his peccadillos, which run twelve lines of verse along the poem (14, 315-330, p. 302). This is a very beautiful passage to see the gods in happy harmony. I continue along in this part because Hera accepts the invitation if they go to her chamber, so as not to be seen by the other gods, to which Zeus replies:

> *'Hera, do not fear that any mortal or any god*
> *will see, so close shall be the golden cloud that I gather*
> *about us. Not even Helios can look at us through it,*
> *although beyond all others his light has the sharpest vision.'*
>
> (14. 342-345, p. 303)

> *There they lay down together and drew about them a golden*
> *wonderful cloud, and from it the glimmering dew descended.'*
>
> (350-351, p. 303)

So the god that knows it all does it all.

10

The Goddess Helps the Hero

In *The Valkyrie*, second act, scene 1, Wotan greets his daughter Brünnhilde and orders her to help his incestuous son, the Wälsung Siegmund, in the coming fight against Hunding, Sieglinde's husband.

Wotan:

> *Go bridle your horse,*
> *warrior maid!*
> *Seize your shield;*
> *battle is near.*
> *Brünnhilde's off to the fight,*
> *the Wälsung is victor today!*
> *Hunding falls to him;*
> *leave him to lie;*
> *for Walhall he is not fit.*
> *So hasten away,*
> *ride to the field!*

> (*Valkyrie*, act 2, scene 1, pp. 96-97)

Wotan and Fricka had had an encounter in act 2, scene 1 of *The Valkyrie* (already referred to in this work) during which Fricka convinces him that Siegmund is not the independent agent he's looking for. Wotan needs a free agent to rescue the cursed ring now in the hands of the giant Fafner who, transformed into a dragon

with the help of the magic tarnhelm, lives in a cave. After this fight
with Fricka, Wotan will reverse his initial order to Brünnhilde.

Brünnhilde:

> *Fricka*
> *has won the fight;*
> *since she smiles at the outcome.*
> *Father, what news*
> *have you to tell me?*
> *Why this sadness and sorrow?*
>
> (*Valkyrie*, act 2, scene 2, p. 105)

> *But the Wälsung, Siegmund,*
> *is he not free?*
>
> (p. 110)

Wotan:

> *The lie was revealed*
> *when Fricka appeared:*
> *I stood ashamed;*
> *I had no reply!*
> *So to her I had to surrender.*

Brünnhilde:

> *Then Siegmund must fall in his fight?*
>
> (p. 110)

Wotan:

> *Fight boldly for Fricka,*
> *guardian of wedlock's vow!*

The choice she made,
that choice must be mine:
my own desires are but useless.
Since that free one I cannot fashion,
be Fricka's champion,
fight for her slave!

(pp. 111-112)

You must conquer Siegmund,
and Hunding must win in the fight!
Guard yourself well,
be stern and strong;
bring all your boldness
and force to the fight:
a strong sword
has Siegmund;
he'll not easily yield!

(p. 112)

Brünnhilde is not quite ready to obey this command; Wotan loves Siegmund, and so does she. Brünnhilde comes to announce to Siegmund that he will die today, and he will go to Walhall. He resists to go and even threatens to kill Sieglinde with his sword.

Brünnhilde:

Oh stay, Wälsung!
Hear what I say!
Sieglinde lives then—
and Siegmund lives by her side!
The choice is mine;
and fate is altered;
you, Siegmund,
take my blessing, and win!

Your sword shall be true,
and the Valkyrie is true as well!
  Farewell, Siegmund,
    hero I love!
I will meet you there in the battle!

(*Valkyrie*, act 2, scene 5, p. 122)

But to no avail. In act 2, scene 5 (p. 125), Wotan will shatter Siegmund's sword in the battle; and disarmed, Hunding kills him. Afterward, under Wotan's order, with a single movement of his spear, Hunding falls dead to the ground. This is the last we see of him in *The Ring* or anywhere else for that matter. Brünnhilde has to flee to avoid Wotan's rage (*The Valkyrie*, act 2, scene 5, p. 125).

In *The Iliad*, Achilleus gets the help of the gods in many occasions; but most important of all is the help he receives from the goddess Pallas Athene at the very moment when he is fighting Hektor. Summoned by Zeus, Athene appeared in the middle of the fight:

But the goddess grey-eyed Athene came now to Peleion
and stood close beside him and addressed him in winged words: 'Beloved
of Zeus, shining Achilleus, I am hopeful now that you and I
will take back great glory to the ships of the Achaians, after
we have killed Hektor, for all his slakeless fury for battle.
Now there is no way for him to get clear away from us,
not though Apollo who strikes from afar should be willing to undergo
much, and wallow before our father Zeus of the aegis.

He was eyeing Hektor's splendid body, to see where it might best
give way, ...

(22. 214-221, p. 441)

. . . . where the collar-bones hold the neck from the shoulders,
the throat, where death of the soul comes more swiftly; in this place
brilliant Achilleus drove the spear as he came on in fury,
and clean through the soft part of the neck the spearpoint was driven.
Yet the ash-spear heavy with bronze did not severe the windpipe,
so that Hektor could still make exchange of words spoken.

(324-329, p. 444)

Then, dying, Hektor of the shining helmet spoke to him:

'Be careful now; for I might be made into the gods' curse
upon you, on that day when Paris and Phoibos Apollo
destroy you in the Skaian gates, for all your valour.'

(22. 355, 358-360, p. 444)

Other heroes are also protected by the gods: in fact, the gods are continually merged with the mortals. In the fight between Menelaos and Paris to decide who would win Helen of Argos, Aphrodite comes to the rescue of Paris while Athene was helping Menelaos. Menelaos had gotten hold of Paris' helmet and was about to strangle him:

Now he would have dragged him away and won glory forever
had not Aphrodite daughter of Zeus watched sharply.
She broke the chinstrap, made from the hide of a slaughtered bullock,
and the helmet came away empty in the heavy hand of Atreides.

(3. 373-376, p. 110)

. . . . But Aphrodite caught up Paris
easily, since she was divine, and wrapped him in a thick mist
and set him down again in his own perfumed bedchamber.

(380-382, p. 110)

After the fight mentioned above, Paris turned to Helen once in the bedchamber:

> *'Lady, censure my heart no more in bitter reprovals.*
> *This time Menelaos with Athene's help has beaten me;*
> *another time I shall beat him. We have gods on our side also.*
> *Come, then, rather let us go to bed and turn to love-making.'*
> (438-441, p. 112)

In council, Zeus spoke to Hera in anger:

> *'Two among the goddesses stand by Menelaos,*
> *Hera of Argos, and Athene who stands by her people.*
> *Yet see, here they are sitting apart, looking on at the fighting,*
> *and take their pleasure. Meanwhile laughing Aphrodite forever*
> *stands by her man and drives the spirits of death away from him.*
> *Even now she has rescued him when he thought he would perish.*
> *So, the victory now is with warlike Menelaos.'*
> (4. 7-13. p. 113)

11

Anger/Rage

In *The Ring of the Nibelung*, the anger and rage is that of Wotan pursuing and scolding Brünnhilde after her disobedience.

He comes out from the pinewood in a towering rage and strides to the group of Valkyries on the height, looking around for Brünnhilde.

Wotan:

> *Where is Brünnhild?*
> *Where is the guilty one?*
> *Can you be daring*
> *to hide her from me?*

(*Valkyrie*, act 3, scene 2, p. 139)

Wotan:

> *No more will you ride from Walhall;*
> *no more will you choose*
> *heroes who fall;*
> *or bring me the warriors*
> *who guard my hall;*
> *and in Walhall, when we are feasting,*
> *no more shall you fill*
> *my drink—horn for me;*
> *no more may I kiss*

the mouth of my child;
the host of the gods
no more shall know you;
cast for ever
from the clan of the gods.
You broke the bond of our love,
and from my sight, henceforth, Brünnhild
                                        [is banned!
                                (pp. 141-142)

Wotan's rage will be transformed into paternal love in his moving farewell to Brünnhilde.

In *The Iliad*, anger and rage are already present in the first line of the poem.

Sing, goddess, the anger of Peleus' son Achilleus
and its devastation, which put pains thousandfold upon the
     Achaians,
hurled in their multitudes to the house of Hades strong souls
of heroes, but gave their bodies to be the delicate feasting
of dogs, of all birds, and the will of Zeus was accomplished
since that time when first there stood in division of conflict
Atreus' son the lord of men and brilliant Achilleus.
                                (1. 1-7, p. 59)

Achilleus' rage is directed to King Agamemnon who abducted his girl Briseis. This rage is going to last through most of *The Iliad*. At one point, Agamemnon tries to placate Achilleus' anger by offering him back his girls and other splendid gifts.

Agamemnon:

> *And let him choose for himself twenty of the Trojan women*
> *who are the loveliest of all after Helen of Argos.*
> (9. 139-140, pp 201-202)

Achilleus refuses Agamemnon's gifts.

Achilleus:

> *I will join with him in no counsel, and in no action.*
> *He cheated me and he did me hurt. Let him not beguile me*
> *with words again. This is enough for him. Let him of his own will*
> *be damned, since Zeus of the counsels has taken his wits away from him.*
> *I hate his gifts. I hold him light as the strip of a splinter.*
> *Not if he gave me ten times as much, and twenty times over*
> *as he possesses now, not if more should come to him from elsewhere,*
> (374-380, p. 208)

> *So long as Hektor was still alive, and Achilleus was angry,*
> *so long as the citadel of lord Priam was a city untaken,*
> *for this time the great wall of the Achaians stood firm.*
> (12. 10-12, p. 258)

Achilleus does come into the fighting and in time kills Hektor, who, in turn, had killed Patroklos, Achilleus's beloved friend and companion. After Patroklos's death, Achilleus:

> *Now I am making an end of my anger. It does not become me*
> *unrelentingly to rage on. Come, then! The more quickly*

drive on the flowing-haired Achaians into the fighting,
so that I may go up against the Trojans, and find out
if they still wish to sleep out beside the ships.

(19. 67-71, p. 394)

12

The Homeric-Supplicating Gesture

In *The Valkyrie* (act 3, scene 2, p. 142), Brünnhilde lies half kneeling before Wotan, embracing his knees in the Homeric-supplicating gesture while her sisters, the eight Valkyries, are pleading not to punish her after she disobeyed Wotan, her father, and tried to save Siegmund in the fight against Hunding. The god reverses Brünnhilde's action, made the magic sword fall from Siegmund's hands; and, disarmed, Hunding kills him. Now the god decrees his punishment.

Wotan:

> *In long, deep sleep*
> *you shall be bound:*
> *the man who wakes you again,*
> *that man awakes you as wife!*
>
> (*Valkyrie*, act 3, scene 3, p. 149)

Later on, Brünnhilde—still embracing Wotan's knees, as called in the libretto (and as shown in the Harry Kupfer production of *The Valkyrie* that I saw in the Berlin Staatsoper in the year 2002)—will plead with the god to grant her one more thing. The god will grant her a flame to surround the rock where she sleeps so that only a hero without fear who can pass through the flame can awaken her.

He raises her from her knees and prepares to say good-bye to his favorite daughter in one of the tenderest moments of the entire *Ring*. He calls the god Loge to kindle the fire and leaves his daughter:

Wotan:

> *Only the man*
> *who braves my spear-point*
> *can pass through this sea of flame!*
>
> (p. 152)

'Then he gazes sorrowfully back at Brünnhilde, turns slowly and departs' (Porter, p. 152). The god feels sad. The man who braves the fire will be Siegfried, the hero of the second opera of the *Ring of the Nibelung*: *Siegfried*.

Embracing the knees in *The Iliad*.

In *The Iliad*, we find Thetis, daughter of Zeus, mother of Achilleus:

> *She came and sat beside him with her left hand embracing*
> *his knees, but took him underneath the chin with her right hand*
> *and spoke in supplication to lord Zeus son of Kronos:*
> *'Father Zeus, if ever before in war or action*
> *I did you favour among the immortals, now grant what I ask for.*
> *Now give honour to my son short-lived beyond all other*
> *mortals. Since even now the lord of men Agamemnon*
> *dishonours him, who has taken away his prize and keeps it.*
> *Zeus of the counsels, lord of Olympos, now do him honour.*
> *So long put strength into the Trojans, until the Achaians*
> *give my son his rights, and his honour is increased among them.'*
>
> (1. 500-510, p. 72)

Thetis complains that Agamemnon has taken away from Achilleus the woman Briseis, who had been given him as a prize after they sacked Thebe. This enraged Achilleus, and he decided not to fight with the Achaians; he who was the bravest of the figthers withdrew from fighting. (This is the beginning of *The Iliad*.) Thetis asks Zeus to honor Achilleus by favoring the Trojans in the fight. He promised to do so:

> '. . . . *I will look to these things that they will be accomplished.*
> *See then, I will bend my head that you may believe me.*'
>   (523-524, p. 73)

13

The God Gives His Beloved Daughter to a Mortal

The Valkyrie Brünnhilde has disobeyed her father, the god Wotan. She is to leave Walhall and to receive a very serious punishment: He will put her to sleep, high on a mountain rock. In a long farewell, Wotan will sing to his beloved daughter:

> *These radiant, glorious eyes,*
> *which, smiling, often I kissed,*
> > *when courage*
> > *I acclaimed with kisses,*
>
> *yes, these gleaming, radiant eyes,*
> *which shone so bright in the storm,*
>
> > *On some happy mortal*
> > *one day they will shine:*
> *but I, hapless immortal,*
> *I must lose them forever.*
> > *And sadly*
> > *the god must depart;*
> *my kiss takes your godhead away!*
>
> (*Valkyrie*, act 3, scene 3, p. 151)

Kissing her eyes, the god takes her divinity away. She will awake as a mortal woman in the opera *Siegfried*.

In *The Iliad*, Thetis comes to the house of the famous smith Hephaistos (son of Zeus) to ask for a new armor for Achilleus. Patroklos was wearing Achilleus's shield and helmet when he was killed by Hektor, and the latter took both items with him. Thetis will complain to Hephaistos, among other things, that Zeus gave her in marriage to a mortal man:

> 'Hephaistos, is there among all the goddesses on Olympos
> one who in her heart has endured so many grim sorrows
> as the griefs Zeus, son of Kronos, has given me beyond others?
> Of all the other sisters of the sea he gave me to a mortal,
> to Peleus, Aiakos' son, and I had to endure mortal marriage
> though much against my will. And now he, broken by mournful
> old age, lies away in his halls. Yet I have other troubles.'
>
> (18. 429-435, p. 386)

And she proceeded to explain her sorrows and Achilleus's predicament and rage against Agamemnom; then, finally, she asked Hephaistos for the new armor for Achilleus. I take upon myself the liberty to make a digression here. Hephaistos gave orders to his fellows, twenty of them, to start working; and "the work went on." Hephaistos made a shield of splendor, bronze, tin, gold, silver the description of which in the poem takes up lines 475 to 607 of book 18 of *The Iliad* (p. 391). The remaining lines, 608-616, are taken by the description of the massive helmet he made for Achilleus. The hero, so attired with new weapons, decided to enter battle against the Trojans in book 19.

On a Sunday morning, while reading *The Iliad* and writing these notes, I am also listening to Wagner's *Tristan und Isolde* (Waltraud Meier, Siegfried Jerusalem, and Daniel Barenboim conducting the Berliner Philarmoniker, Teldec).

Second act:

> *O sink hernieder,*   *Sink down upon us,*
> *Nacht der Liebe,*   *night of love*
> *gib Vergessen,*   *make me forget,*
> *löse von*   *free me*
> *der Welt mich los!*   *from the world!*

Overpowered by the combined very strong emotions, marveling at the artistry of these two geniuses of mankind, I had to stop writing and got up from my chair to take a rest. After a moment, I did not know from where the strongest emotions came: whether from Wagner or from Homer. I leave it at that.

Figure 5: Photo of the Festspielhaus

Figure 6: Members of the Asociación Wagner de Venezuela
   in Bayreuth. In the background, the balcony where the
   fanfare is played, which announces the beginning of
   the opera and of each act. Author in front row, second
   from right.

Figure 7: Richard Wagner's portrait.

Figure 8: The cast of the premiere of *The Ring*, Bayreuth, 1876.

Figure 9: Plate in front of the house where Wagner was born—Leipzig, 1813

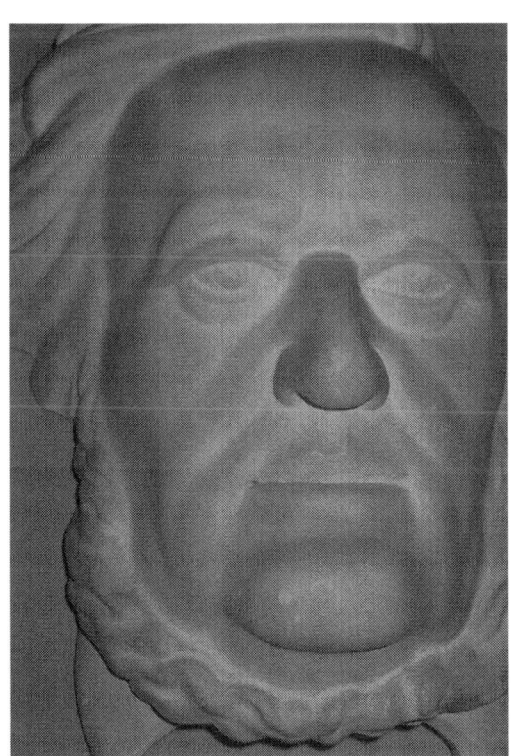

Figure 10: Wagner's face mask.

14

Brünnhilde's Fate

When Wotan is announcing Brünnhilde her punishment because she tried to veer the fight of Siegmund and Hunding in favor of the former, Wotan will sentence that she will be banished from her sisters, the other eight Valkyries; and she will be put to sleep—a long sleep—on the rocks. When she awakes, she will sit and spin as all the mortal women do.

Wotan:

> *A husband will gain*
> *all her womanly grace;*
> *that masterful husband*
> *will make her obey;*
> *she'll sit and spin by the fire,*
> *and the world will deride her fate!*
> (*Valkyrie*, act 3, scene 2, p. 143)

In *The Iliad*, weaving is what women do all the time; in this instance, the messenger Iris appears:

> *She came on Helen in the chamber; she was weaving a great web,*
> *a red folding robe, and working into it the numerous struggles*
> *of Trojans, breakers of horses, and bronze-armoured Achaians,*
> *struggles that they endured for her sake at the hands of the war god.*
> (2. 125-128, p. 103)

Another occasion—this time, the weaver is Hekabe, Hektor's mother:

> *There lay the elaborately wrought robes, the work of Sidonian women, whom Alexandros himself, the godlike, had brought home from the land of Sidon, crossing the wide sea, on that journey when he brought back also gloriously descended Helen.*
>
> (6. 289-292, p. 161)

And again,

> *while Helen of Argos was sitting among her attendant women directing the magnificent work done by her handmaidens.*
>
> (323-324, p. 161)

15

Farewells to the Beloved

In *The Ring*, Wotan says good-bye to his beloved daughter Brünnhilde in a rather long, moving, and deeply felt farewell. The farewell represents, both in its text and musically, one of the highest dramatic moments of the entire Tetralogy.

Wotan (raising her from her knees and gazing with emotion into her eyes):

> *Farewell, my valiant,*
> *   glorious child!*
> *You were the holiest pride of my heart!*
> *Farewell! Farewell! Farewell!*
> *   Though I must leave you,*
> *   and may no longer*
> *embrace you in greeting;*
> *   though you may no more*
> *   ride beside me,*
> *nor bear my mead in Walhall;*
> *   though I abandon you*
> *   whom I love so,*
> *the laughing delight of my eye:*
> *   a bridal fire*
> *   shall blaze to protect you,*
> *as never has burned for a bride.*
>
> *(Valkyrie*, act 3, scene 3, p 150-151)

Wotan places Brünnhilde on a rock where she will sleep for a long time. When she awakens in the opera *Siegfried*, she will be a mortal woman. Wotan will summon Loge again to light the fire around the rock:

> *Loge, hear!*
> *Come at my call!*
>
> *Arise! Come, flickering Loge;*
> *surround the rock, ring it with flame!*

Loge appears as a flame and kindles the fire, which Wotan spreads with his spear around the rock:

> *Only the man*
> *who braves my spear-point*
> *can pass through this sea of flame!*
>
> (act 2, scene 3, p. 152)

The god slowly departs. He looks "sorrowfully" at Brünnhilde. The god feels sadness.

In *The Iliad*, Andromache to Hektor, her husband, before he goes to battle:

> *Hektor smiled in silence as he looked on his son, but she,*
> *Andromache, stood close beside him, letting her tears fall,*
> *and clung to his hand and called him by name and spoke to him: 'Dearest,*
> *your own great strength will be your death, and you have no pity*
> *on your little son, nor on me, ill-starred, who soon must be your widow;*
> *for presently the Achaians, gathering together,*
> *will set upon you and kill you; and for me it would be far better*
> *to sink into the earth when I have lost you, for there is no other*

consolation for me after you have gone to your destiny—
only grief; since I have no father, no honoured mother.'
(6. 404-413, p. 164)

Hektor answered her:

But it is not so much the pain to come of the Trojans
that troubles me, not even of Priam the king nor Hekabe,
not the thought of my brothers who in their numbers and valour
shall drop in the dust under the hands of men who hate them,
as troubles me the thought of you, when some bronze-armoured
Achaian leads you off, taking away your day of liberty,
in tears; and in Argos you must work at the loom of another.
(450-456, p. 165)

'Poor Andromache! Why does your heart sorrow so much for me?
No man is going to hurl me to Hades, unless it is fated,
but as for fate, I think that no man yet has escaped it
once it has taken its first form, neither brave man nor coward.
Go therefore back to our house, and take up your own work . . . .'
(486-490, p. 166)

Andromache's farewell when she learns Hektor has died:

But she, when she breathed again and the life was gathered back into her,
lifted her voice among the women of Troy in mourning:
'Hektor, I grieve for you. You and I were born to a single
destiny, you in Troy in the house of Priam, and I
in Thebe, underneath the timbered mountain of Plakos
in the house of Eëtion, who cared for me when I was little,
ill-fated he, I ill-starred. I wish he had never begotten me.
Now you go down to the house of Death in the secret places
of the earth, and left me here behind in the sorrow of mourning,

a widow in your house, and the boy is only a baby
who was born to you and me, the unfortunate. You cannot help him,
Hektor, any more, since you are dead. Nor can he help you.'
                                           (22. 475-486, p. 448)

So she spoke, in tears; and the women joined in her mourning.
                                           (515, p. 449)

16

The Gods' Council

This is another element of resemblance between *The Ring* and *The Iliad*. In *The Twilight of the Gods*, there occurs the following: Brünnhilde's sister, Waltraute, comes to visit her on the rock, where she lives surrounded by fire, and tells her how their father, Wotan, sits in the hall in Walhall assembled in council with all the gods and the heroes, waiting until the ring of the Nibelung, now in Brünnhilde's hands, is returned to the river, to the Rhine's daughters, and the curse will pass. When Siegfried married Brünnhilde, he gave her the ring as a token of his love. She gave him her horse, Grane, and sent him out to search for adventures in the world. Brünnhilde refuses to part with the ring (Porter, act 1, scene 3, pp. 273-274).

Waltraute:

> *The holy clan*
> *came as he called them;*
> *and Wotan, on high,*
> *took his place.*
> *By his side*
> *in fear and dismay they assembled;*
> *in ranks around the hall*
> *he stationed his heroes.*
> *He sits there,*
> *speaks no word,*

enthroned in silence,
stern and sad;
the spear in splinters
grasped in his hand.
                    (*Twilight of the Gods*, act 1, scene 3, p. 274)

In *The Iliad*, the god of gods, Zeus, also sits frequently in his halls in the Olympos surrounded by all the gods holding councils to deliver matters of importance:

> *Now the gods at the side of Zeus were sitting in council*
> *over the golden floor, and among them the goddess Hebe*
> *poured them nectar as wine, while they in the golden drinking-cups*
> *drank to each other, gazing down on the city of the Trojans.*
>   (4. 1-4, p. 113)

> *Then Zeus himself of the wide brows took his place on the golden*
> *throne, as underneath his feet tall Olympos was shaken.*
>   (8. 442-443, p. 194)

17

Prophecies

In *The Ring*, there is a forest bird, the woodbird, which gives messages (prophecies) to Siegfried. I like to think that these messages come from the god Wotan.

Siegfried:

> *You lovely woodbird,*
> *how sweet is your song:*
> *here in the wood is your home?*
> *I wish I could understand you!*
> *I'm sure you've something to tell—*
> *perhaps of a loving mother?*
>
> (*Siegfried*, act 2, scene 2, p. 202)

At first, Siegfried tries to imitate the sound of the bird by making a pipe from some reeds (p. 203); later, in the next scene, he understands what the bird sings and interprets it. Siegfried has killed the dragon Fafner and smeared his hand with blood; involuntarily, he puts his finger to his mouth to suck the blood. That makes him wise. "It seems the woodbirds are speaking to me." In effect, the woodbird tells him of the Nibelung hoard; the magic tarnhelm; and the magic ring, which he will soon claim. (p. 207)

Later, again the woodbird will prophesize:

> *Who wakens the maid,*
> *Brünnhild the bride,*
> *no coward can be:*
> *one unacquainted with fear!*
>
> (scene 3, p. 218)

The woodbird will lead him toward the rock; encircled by flames, Brünnhilde awaits to be awakened by the hero unacquainted with fear (*Siegfried*, act 3, scene 3, p. 232-244).

In *The Iliad*, there is also a bird interpreter of the gods (Kalchas), and prophecies are involved:

> *He spoke thus and sat down again, and among them stood up*
> *Kalchas, Thestor's son, far the best of the bird interpreters,*
> *who knew all things that were, the things to come and the things past,*
> *who guided into the land of Ilion the ships of the Achaians*
> *through that seercraft of his own that Phoibos Apollo gave him.*
>
> (1. 68-72, p. 61)

18

The Norns

In the prelude of *The Twilight of the Gods*, there appear the three Norns; they represent past, present, and future. They are the daughters of Erda (the goddess of the earth) who weave the rope of destiny, tying it into the pine tree until it breaks at the end of the prelude (pp. 247-252).

The Norns call to each other, "Sing, sister," and so they do, taking turns to sing a miniversion of the saga of Wotan, that is, from the time Wotan came to drink at the spring, where he lost an eye, and broke a branch of the world ash tree to make his spear. This took place before we encounter Wotan for the first time in scene 2 of *Rhinegold*.

They continue unfolding the story of Wotan, ruler of the world, with his gods and his heroes until the present time when the dejected god sits in his hall waiting for the darkness to fall on the gods after his spear was shattered by young Siegfried. There, he waits, surrounded by the branches of the world ash tree, which he has ordered cut and piled around the Walhall to burn it. "Sing and spin the cord, sisters" until the tangled and frail cord splits. By then, the end is on the way after the immolation of Brünnhilde at Siegfried's pyre when the fire will reach Walhall and consume the gods and all. The end of the gods has come (*Twilight of the Gods*, prelude, pp. 247-252).

In *The Iliad*, the command is issued from the beginning of the poem, I presume, by the poet himself:

> *Sing, goddess, the anger of Peleus' son Achilleus*
> *and its devastation, which put pains thousandfold upon the*
>   *Achaians,*
> *hurled in their multitudes to the house of Hades strong souls*
> *of heroes, but gave their bodies to be the delicate feasting*
> *of dogs, of all birds, and the will of Zeus was accomplished*
> *since that time when first there stood in division of conflict*
> *Atreus' son the lord of men and brilliant Achilleus.*
>
> (1.1-7, p. 59)

And the singing unfolds, giving us an account of the very many fights and encounters and battles between its heroes until we come to the burial of Hektor, some 15,693 verses further along (24. 804, p. 496).

19

Sleep You, Hagen, My Son?

Hagen is guarding the castle of the Gibichungs while Siegfried and Gunther (Hagen's half brother) are on a mission to bring Brünnhilde back to marry Gunther while Siegfried will marry Gunther's sister Gutrune. Alberich appears crouching before Hagen, leaning his arms on Hagen's knees, the Homeric-supplicating position.

Alberich:

> *Sleep you, Hagen, my son?*
> *You sleep, and hear me not;*
> *through sleep I lost my power!*
> > (*Twilight of the Gods*, act 2, scene 1, pp. 281-282)

Alberich is to remind Hagen that the gods are due for destruction and that he should destroy Siegfried who now possesses the cursed ring.

Alberich:

> *The golden ring,*
> *that ring—you have to win it!*

> (p. 283)

Wake from your slumber,
strive for the ring!

Though you were too weak
to fight with the giant,
whom only Siegfried could slay,
yet deadly hatred
I bred in Hagen
so he could avenge me;
the ring he'll win me,
though Wälsung and Wotan conspire!
Swear to me, Hagen, my son!

Crafty hero! Be true!
Be true! True!

(p. 284)

Then Alberich disappears.

In *The Iliad*:

King Agamemnon speaks:

Hear me, friends: in my sleep a Dream divine came to me
through the immortal night, and in appearance and stature
and figure it most closely resembled splendid Nestor.
It came and stood above my head and spoke a word to me:
'Son of wise Atreus breaker of horses, are you sleeping?
He should not sleep night long who is a man burdened with counsels
and responsibility for a people and cares so numerous.'

(2. 56-62, p. 77)

20

Offerings to the Gods

Offerings to the gods have taken place since ancient times. All the great civilizations of antiquity carried such rituals; hence, among the Greeks, and in the kingdom of Wotan, among the Gibichungs, such offerings were also observed. When Siegfried returns from his visit to Brünnhilde's rock, where he had gone to woo the maiden to gain her as a bride for Gunther, there occurs a big celebration with offerings to the gods. They are to prepare for the wedding of Brünnhilde to Gunther.

Hagen mounts on a high rock and sounds his horn:

> *Hoiho! Hoihohoho!*
> *You Gibich vassals,*
> *answer my call.*
> *(Twilight of the Gods, act 2, scene 3, p. 288)*

Later, Hagen proceeds to announce the offerings:

> *Sacred oxen*
> *must be slaughtered;*
> *on Wotan's altar*
> *pour forth their blood!*
>
> *Take a boar as offering,*
> *kill it for Froh;*

and a goat in its prime
strike down for Donner!
Sheep should then
be slaughtered for Fricka,
and then she will smile on this wedding!

(p. 290)

The vassals (first time that Wagner uses a chorus in *The Ring of the Nibelung*):

After these offerings,
what next should we do?

Hagen:

Your drinkhorns take,
and ask your women
to fill with wine,
until they are full!

So goes the celebration and offerings to the gods to greet the maiden, Brünnhilde.

Hagen:

Now stop your laughter,
faithful vassals!
Receive Gunther's bride!
Brünnhilde soon shall be here.

(p. 290-291)

In *The Iliad*. Hekabe, King Priam's queen, mother of Hektor goes to present a gift of a beautiful robe to the goddess Athene. She is accompanied by a group of noble women:

When these had come to Athene's temple on the peak of the citadel,
Theano of the fair cheeks opened the door for them, daughter
of Kisseus, and wife of Antenor, breaker of horses,
she whom the Trojans had established to be Athene's priestess.
With a wailing cry all lifted up their hands to Athene,
and Theano of the fair cheeks taking up the robe laid it
along the knees of Athene the lovely haired, and praying
she supplicated the daughter of powerful Zeus: 'Oh lady,
Athene, our city's defender, shining among goddesses:
break the spear of Diomedes, and grant that the man be
hurled on his face in front of the Skaian gates; so may we
instantly dedicate within your shrine twelve heifers,
yearlings, never broken, if only you will have pity
on the town of Troy, and the Trojan wives and their innocent children.'
She spoke in prayer, but Pallas Athene turned her head from her.

(6. 297-311, p. 161)

21

Funeral Pyres

In *The Ring*, there is a funeral pyre for the dead hero Siegfried. He had been killed by the Gibichung Hagen during a hunting trip. The deed had been planned by Brünnhilde and Hagen. They had decided Siegfried was a traitor because he arranged the marriage of King Gunther, half brother of Hagen, to Brünnhilde, the latter already being his wife; then, in turn, Siegfried will marry Gutrune. The promise had taken place while Siegfried was under the effect of a potion that made him forget Brünnhilde.

Hagen:

> *No hand can help,*
> *no deed can atone,*
> *but only—Siegfried's death.*
> > (*Twilight of the Gods*, act 2, scene 5, p. 302)

Siegfried had betrayed Brünnhilde and had also broken the blood brotherhood pact he had consummated with Gunther.

Brünnhilde:

> *He betrayed you;*   (to Gunther and Hagen)
> *and me—you all have betrayed me!*

> *If I had my rights,*
> *all the blood of the world*
> *could not revenge me for your crime!*
> *So the death of one*
> *now must content me:*
> *Siegfried's death*
> *atones for his crime, and yours!*
>
> (pp. 302-303)

Brünnhilde orders to prepare the funeral pyre for Siegfried:

> *Sturdy branches,*
> *building his pyre*
> *now bring to the shore of the Rhine!*
> *Bright and clear,*
> *kindle the flame:*
>
> *Obey Brünnhild's command!*
>
> (act 3, scene 5, p. 325)

In *The Iliad*, there is a funeral pyre for the hero Patroklos, beloved companion of Achilleus, who was killed by Hektor.

Achilleus speaking at the pyre:

> *'Good-bye, Patroklos. I hail you even in the house of the death god*
> *For all that I promised you in time past I am accomplishing.*
> *Here are twelve noble sons of the great-hearted Trojans*
> *whom the fire feeds on, all, as it feeds on you. But I will not*
> *give Hektor, Priam's son, to the fire, but the dogs, to feast on.'*
>
> (23. 179-183, p. 455)

Achilleus speaking to Agamemnon at the pyre of Patroklos:

> *'Son of Atreus, and you other greatest of all the Achaians,*
> *first put out with gleaming wine the pyre that is burning,*
> *all that still has on it the fury of fire; and afterwards*
> *we shall gather up the bones of Patroklos, the son of Menoitios.'*
>
> (236-239, p. 456)

In *The Iliad*, there is also a funeral pyre for the hero Hektor. King Priam of Troy rescued the body of his son Hektor from Achilleus and asked the men of Troy to prepare Hektor's funeral pyre:

> *He spoke, and they harnessed to the wagons their mules and their oxen*
> *and presently were gathered in front of the city. Nine days*
> *they spent bringing in an endless supply of timber. But when*
> *the tenth dawn had shone forth with her light upon mortals,*
> *they carried out bold Hektor, weeping, and set the body*
> *aloft a towering pyre for burning. And set fire to it.*
>
> (24. 782-787, p. 496)

22

Guiding Birds/Birds of Omen

In *The Twilight of the Gods*, Brünnhilde sings, addressing Wotan, still holding council in Walhall and tells him:

> *Call back your ravens*
> *hovering round me;*
> *they'll bring to you those tidings*
> *you have both feared and desired.*
> *Rest now, rest now, O god!*
> > (*Twilight of the Gods*, act 2, scene 3. p. 326)

Farther along:

> *Fly home, you ravens!*
> *tell your Lord the tidings*
> *that here by the Rhine you have learned!*
> *Past Brünnhilde's mountain*
> *take your flight,*
> *where Loge is burning!*
> *Summon Loge to Walhall!*
> *For the gods' destruction*
> *soon shall be here.*
> *I cast now the flame*
> *at Walhall's glorious height.*
> > (scene 3, p. 327)

Wagner's instructions indicate that she seizes a great fire-brand from one of the vassals and flings the brand on the pyre where Siegfried rests. Two ravens fly up to the shore and disappear in the background. At the end she mounts her horse Grane and leaps with a single bound into the blazing pyre. With her goes the ring that will be recovered from the river by the Rhinemaidens; the river overflows. Walhall burns, and everything turns ablaze. At the end, everything burns, and a cloud of smoke floats over the remains. The Rhinemaidens now recover the ring cleansed from its curse. The end of the gods has come to pass. (*Twilight of the Gods*, pp. 327-329).

In *The Iliad* there also appear birds with missions. During King Priam's trip to visit Achilleus to ask for the body of his dead son Hektor whom Achilleus had killed, Hekabe, Priam's wife, tells him:

> *Make your prayer then to the dark-misted, the son of Kronos*
> *on Ida, who looks out on all the Troad, and ask him*
> *for a bird of omen, a rapid messenger, which to his own mind*
> *is dearest of all birds and his strength is the biggest, one seen*
> *on the right, so that once your eyes have rested upon him*
> *you can trust in him and go to the ships of the fast-mounted Danaans.*
> (24. 290-295, p. 483)

> *So he spoke in prayer, and Zeus of the counsels heard him.*
> *Straightway he sent down the most lordly of birds, an eagle,*
> *the dark one, the marauder, called as well the black eagle.*
> (314-316, p. 483)

> *. . . . He swept through the city*
> *appearing on the right hand, and the people looking upon him*
> *were uplifted and the hearts made glad in the breasts of all of them.*
>   (319-321, p. 483)

The difference is that in *The Ring*, the ravens are birds of bad omen: the destruction of Walhall and the end of the gods, while in *The Iliad*, the eagle is a good omen.

23

Offerings to the Funeral Pyres

In *The Ring,* Brünnhilde will offer the cursed ring to the pyre:

> *My heritage*
> *I claim from the hero.*
> *Accursed gold!*
> *Terrible ring!*
> *My hand grasps you*
> *to cast you away.*

> *you Rhinemaidens who dwell in the waters,*
> *I shall obey your advice.*
> *What you desire*
> *I'll give to you:*
> *and from my ashes*
> *gather your treasure!*
> *This fire, burning my frame,*
> *cleanses the curse from the ring!*
> *There in the Rhine,*
> *the ring shall be pure;*
> *preserve it,*
> *and guard your shining gold*
> *whose theft has cursed all our woe.*
> (*Twilight of the Gods,* act 3, scene 3, pp. 326-327)

Brünnhilde herself jumps into Siegfried's pyre with her horse Grane in an act of supreme immolation.

Brünnhilde:

> *Grane, my horse!*
> *I greet my friend!*
> *Can you tell, my friend,*
> *to where I must lead you?*
> *In fiery glory*
> *blazes your lord,*
> *Siegfried, my hero and love.*
> *To follow your master.*
> *Oh! Are you neighing?*
>
>
> *I too am yearning*
> *to join him there;*
> *glorious radiance*
> *has seized on my heart.*
> *I shall embrace him,*
> *united with him,*
> *in sacred yearning,*
> *with him ever one!*
> *Hiayoho! Grane!*
> *Ride to your master!*
> *Siegfried! Siegfried! See!*
> *Brünnhild greets you as wife!*

(pp. 327-328)

Those are her last words before "she mounts her horse and leaps with a single bound into the blazing pyre" before the disaster of the fire comes, engulfing pyre and all Valhall.

In *The Iliad*, offering to Patroklos's pyre:

> *And now brilliant swift-footed Achilleus remembered one more thing.*
> *He stood apart from the pyre and cut off a lock of fair hair*
> *which he had grown long to give to the river Spercheios, and gazing*
> *in deep distress out over the wine-blue water, he spoke forth:*
>   (23. 140-143, p. 454)

> *I would cut my hair for you and make you a grand and holy*
> *sacrifice of fifty rams consecrate to the waters*
> *of your springs, where is your holy ground and your smoking altar.*
>   (146-148, p. 454)

(He remembered that his father had offered Achilleus's hair to the river when he would return home but Achilleus):

> *'Now, since I do not return to the beloved land of my fathers,*
> *I would give my hair into the keeping of the hero Patroklos.'*
>   (150-151, p. 454)

24

How the Funeral Pyres
Are Put Out

In *The Ring*, the river Rhine overflows and puts the fire of Siegfried's pyre out and cleanses all away. Hagen makes a last attempt to get hold of the ring:

Hagen:

> *Give back the ring!*
>> (*Twilight of the Gods*, act 2, scene 3, p. 329)

Two of the Rhinemaidens will hold him by the neck and drown him. The third one, Flosshilde, recovers the ring. The hall of the gods will also be claimed by the fire. The curtain falls. This is the end of *The Ring of the Nibelung*.

In *The Iliad*, Hektor's funeral pyre was put out with wine, as in Patroklos's case.

> *But when all were gathered to one place and assembled together,*
> *first with gleaming wine they put out the pyre that was burning,*
> *all where the fury of the fire still was in force, and thereafter*
> *the brothers and companions of Hektor gathered the white bones*
> *up, mourning, as the tears swelled and ran down their cheeks.*
>> (24. 790-794, p. 496)

This is barely ten verses prior to the ending of *The Iliad*:

> *They piled up the grave-barrow and went away, and thereafter*
> *assembled in a fair gathering and held a glorious*
> *feast within the house of Priam, king under God's hand.*
> *Such was their burial of Hektor, breaker of horses.*
>
> (801-804, p. 496)

The end of *The Iliad*.

25

Conclusion

I will end these references to situations found in *The Ring* that resemble those in *The Iliad* by saying that my ideas here do not by all means pretend to be exhaustive and made me wonder whether Wagner did look at *The Iliad* while he was composing *The Ring*.

I read both books very carefully, and at times, I read *The Iliad* aloud, trying to bring the proper intonation and rhythm to the hexameter verses. Of course, I had to contend with my Spanish accent mixed into my English. I cannot but wonder at how the work will sound in the voice of seasoned Greek actors in an open theater, or more—in the voice of the bards, who kept reciting the poem throughout the centuries—in Greece.

It has been a very enriching experience for me, searching for *The Ring* in *The Iliad*. The *Ring of the Nibelung* is, for me, the greatest music I have ever heard, just as *The Iliad* is the greatest book I have ever read. I wish more people will turn to study it and to listen to *The Ring* and that more people will come to read *The Iliad* after they read these notes. They will find great pleasure for sure.

I have not mentioned anything about the music of *The Ring*. It is one, two, three, or more books in itself. The greatest music ever written. Wagner changed opera and music, in general, with *The Ring* and his other works. The monumental *Ring* took twenty-five years to be completed. I wish more people would approach this work both as text and, especially, as musical drama, as Wagner called his operas. To listen to *The Ring* requires an involvement from the listener that is not usually demanded when you listen to Italian or French operas. There is always something new to be discovered. You never quite come to "possess" *The Ring*; it always eludes you. There is something to learn every time you see or listen to *The Ring*.

The texts of *The Ring* were written between 1848 and 1852; the music, between 1853 and 1874. These texts were published in 1853 under the title *The Ring of the Nibelung*. Later, in 1863, he wrote the poem "The Nibelungs." The operas were written in this order: *The Death of Siegfried* (1848), which later became the *Twilight of the Gods* (1852); then the *Young Siegfried*, which became *Siegfried* (1851); then the *Valkyrie* and *Rhinegold* (1852). The premiere of *The Ring* took place in 1876, in Bayreuth, Bavaria, Germany, in the theater that Wagner had built to play his operas exclusively. The conductor was Hans Richter. More about this below, in the chapter "The Bayreuth Experience."

It is now over one hundred years since the completion (1874) and the premiere of *The Ring* (1876), and little or nothing has been done to look at *The Ring* in the light of *The Iliad*. This is what I have done through my associations.

At first, I called these notes *The Ring of the Nibelung and The Iliad: A Parallel Reading*, but later, I realized it was more like a search for *The Ring* in *The Iliad*. It is as if *The Ring* were embedded in *The Iliad*, a fragmented, translocated *Ring* at that. That is what I had expected to find (q.e.d.) because for some strange reason, I felt a very strong urge to look at *The Ring* while I was reading *The Iliad*. It is remarkable that some bits of ideas of *The Ring* find resonance in *The Iliad*, or conversely, that bits of ideas of *The Iliad* appear here and there in *The Ring*.

I am a Virgo, and as such, I went into the assignment as if it were a piece of a virological research, looking for clues with picky intentions. I needed to work exclusively with quotations from both books in order to make the parallels more convincing in their original contexts.

Wagner surely knew his *Iliad* very well. He and Cosima read the classics every night after dinner, as I mentioned already in the section "The Classic in Wagner." Of course, it is not possible to say from where all these associations came: the elements from *The Iliad* that appear in *The Ring*. Consciously or unconsciously, those elements ended in the text while Wagner was writing *The Ring of the Nibelung*. Purely coincidental?

I always felt I was indebted to Wagner beyond my admiration and devotion; by writing, rightly or wrongly, these humble and picky notes, I feel I have paid my debt.

26

Generalities about *The Ring* and *The Iliad*

This work does not intend to be a scholarly book. *The Ring* and *The Iliad* are very different works, but because I love them both, I tried to bring them together through my associations—just like that! And why not? I already mentioned how the idea of this work came into my mind, so I shall not repeat it here.

Wagner uses archetypal figures in *The Ring*, the oldest and unchangeable characters, which are endowed with all the virtues and vices of the mortals. Both the mortals and the immortals participate in situations of robbery, murder, perjury, vengeance, incest, hate, lust for power, lust for money, and many more evils—the totality of manifestations of the human condition. The gods intermingle with the mortals in many situations. Authors have remarked that some of the evil aspects of Wotan, like lust for power and riches, are a reflection of the domineering tendencies in Wagner himself. Lust for gold is felt by both Wotan and Alberich. The former loved to recover the ring; but the dwarf Alberich, when cursing the ring, proclaimed that in order to possess it, the person had to renounce love (*Rhinegold*). But love persists in Siegmund and in Sieglinde (*The Valkyrie*), and in Siegfried and Brünnhilde (*Siegfried*).

I like to think that power and love cross each other at one point in *The Ring*, as when Wotan, already decadent as he loses his power, punishes Brünnhilde; and she responds that she disobeyed him and tried to help Siegmund because she learned to love him through Wotan himself:

Brünnhilde:

> *Victory or death,*
> *with Siegmund I'd share it!*
> *One thought possessed me,*
> *and I had no choice!*
> *You, who this love*
> *in my heart inspired,*
> *when you inspired*
> *the Wälsung with your will,*
> *you were not betrayed—*
> *though I broke your command.*
>
> (*Valkyrie*, act 3, scene 3, p. 146)

Most human emotions are present in *The Ring*. Wagner possibly intended to present his characters as portraits of all the human evils of the race, and by seeing themselves so reflected, the humans might be changed somehow in their behavior. He did think that the hero Siegfried was to be the new man for the new race in the new world. He is a rebellious, insolent adolescent who, being very strong, forged his own sword, Notung, and who killed the dwarf Mime (true, Mime was trying to kill him); and, because he was fearless, killed the dragon and got the magic tarnhelm and the magic ring; and, guided by the bird, came to Brünnhilde's rock; and, again, being fearless, crossed the fire, awoke the maiden, and they fell in love and married her. These were the heroic deeds of Siegfried, a very different hero from the Siegfried of *Das Nibelungen Lied*, who went horseback in front of his hordes from town to town, conquering them, and who was a lover of luxurious fabrics and brocades for his costumes (much like Wagner himself) and those of his soldiers, and was very much liked wherever he went. The Siegfried of *The Ring* is also very different from the heroes of *The Iliad*, who were mainly warriors. I concede: Siegfried spent most of his time in *The Twilight of the Gods* under the influence of potions so that he could not work on his mission of being the new man in the new race for the new world. I wonder if Wagner thought of that.

When Siegfried comes out of the forest, a natural and innocent man, and enters the world, the society that he finds is not much different from the one of his ancestors: Wotan, Alberich, and the others. Later, he betrays Brünnhilde and Hagen and will be killed. But Brünnhilde loves him very much and decides to immolate herself at his funeral pyre. She hopes this redemptive act will cleanse the world of its evils. Afterward, there is total destruction, and even the gods die. A new world will come to be, and it has. The last leitmotif that is heard in *The Ring* is the one sung by Sieglinde after she learns from Brünnhilde that she is expecting a child, Siegmund's son (Siegfried). She sings to the exaltation of the miracle of love, signaling that the world humanity should strive for love, and not lust for riches (Alberich), for power (Wotan), or for evil actions or desires (*The Valkyrie*, act 3, scene 1, p. 137-138). She also gives thanks to Brünnhilde for having saved her from Wotan's rage.

Many worlds have come and gone, but is our world any better than it was in Wotan's time? Did Brünnhilde's redemption and redemptive act help any?

If *The Ring* is about lust for power and lust for gold and evil emotions, *The Iliad* is more about war.

In *The Iliad*, the Greek gods have more interrelations with the mortals. In fact, they are constantly behind all human actions, and they determine their outcome, whether in battle or out of it.

The Iliad is basically a story of war, battles, rage, blood, fighting, cruelty, vengeance, some love?

Above all, the Greeks believed in excellence, even excellence in fighting, in the intensity of the fight in which they believed. The prize was the glory to be attained with victory. But they were very cruel and vengeful with their enemies. We witnessed the way Achilleus behaved against the body of Hektor after he killed him. In the Greeks, there is the feeling in the warriors that they must complete the best of their actions in the battles themselves, and the soldiers are always exhorted and motivated to incite them to come to battle with the sense of being victorious.

I have described *The Ring* already somewhere, but I have told little or nothing about *The Iliad*, which is a better-known book. It is basically the war of Troy; of their gods, Zeus, Hera, and the muses; and the other gods and goddesses who at times protected the Greeks or the Trojans according to Zeus's desires. The story of Troy in a few words is as follows:

Prince Alexandros (Paris), son of King Priam and Queen Hekabe, went on a trip to Greece. There, he fell in love with Helen of Argos, the most beautiful woman in Greece and, upon his return to Troy, brought her with him. Helen was the wife of King Menelaos, the brother of King Agamemnon of Crete. Agamemnon was furious and summoned all the kings of Greece to form a fleet to invade Troy, in Asia Minor, and rescue Helen. The fleet was formed: "The fleet of the thousand ships," related in detail in *The Iliad*, book 2, 493-759, pp. 89-96. They sailed to Troy; and the siege of the city lasted ten years, at the end of which the Greeks, with their famous wooden Trojan horse, managed to penetrate the walls of the city and conquer Troy, an episode that is not related in *The Iliad*. Heroes in *The Iliad* are Achilleus, the bravest of the great warriors (but his rage against Agamemnon kept him from fighting much of the time); Hektor, son of Priam and Hekabe, was the leader of the Trojans, was the brother of Paris, and the husband of Andromache; other famous names are Odysseus, Nestor, Patroklos (friend and companion of Achilleus), and many, many more valiant and noble warriors. *The Iliad* is the day-to-day life during the siege of Troy (Ilion), the discussion about battles, their planning, the actual fighting of one man against another or in groups, and, above all, the excellence in the fighting.

I was intent on finding *The Ring* in *The Iliad*. Finding *The Ring* in *The Iliad* was not easy. It was not noticeable on a first reading of the book. I had to go deeply into the poem more than once; it was as if dissecting a nerve in a small dead animal pinned on a wooden block (Zoology I): reading the poem over and over again and, looking for the clues there, turned up small pebbles—shining, glittering, as the gold must have appeared to Alberich in the crevices in between the rocks of the bottom of the river Rhine; and when I threaded them together, they fashioned a ring: Alberich's ring, *The Ring of the Nibelung*.

My associations between these two books may be far-fetched but not necessarily so. Look at the example of "Sleep You, Hagen, My Son?" already referred to above. I think I have looked at *The Ring* in a different way, in a new light that may or may not be relevant but simply different. It has been a fun piece of research for me. I hope many people will turn to look at both works again, above all, to listen to *The Ring of the Nibelung* and that they may be able to attend Bayreuth sometime.

27

Appendix

The Bayreuth Experience

So you want to go to Bayreuth? I don't wish to finish this note without describing the experience of attending *The Ring* cycle in Bayreuth. The Wagner Festival in Bayreuth takes place in the summertime, from July 26 to end of August. A new production of the complete *Ring* is presented every six years; together with *The Ring*, there are a total of seven Wagner operas shown. Three operas are presented when there is no *Ring*, distributed in several cycles repeated through the summer.

The operas are presented in the theater, the Festspielhaus (figure 5), located in the outskirts of Bayreuth, a small medieval town in Bavaria, Germany, near Nuremberg. Wagner's operas are very expensive to produce, so few theaters in the world ever venture to present a complete *Ring*. Isolated operas are seen through the year in many cities in the world. *The Valkyrie* is the most often produced; it contains many instances of beautiful lyrical music and, of course, the famous ride of the Valkyries, which is very well-known among the public.

The beginning of *The Rhinegold* is the creation of the world. The theater is in complete darkness; not a noise is heard. The orchestra is not seen because Wagner designed it hidden in a sunken pit, under the stage. Wagner did not want anything to distract the spectator.

People are sitting quietly, all ears, as in a religious celebration, confined in those small wooden seats, very narrow, without seat or back cushions or armrests; and then slowly, softly at first, the music of *Rhinegold* begins. What emerges is a sustained chord in E-flat major, which runs alone for some sixteen bars. Very eerie, an emotion difficult to explain, the spectator doesn't know where the music is coming from. Slowly, the light begins to appear, very timidly, from the stage; as the world is being created, light is its first manifestation. Those chords continue with the superimposed notes that express the rippling effects of the water of the waves of the river Rhine, and they will continue for up to sixty-six total bars, now in *arpeggios,* which cease when Alberich appears and says, "He! He! You nixies!" Alberich enters after the playful Rhinemaidens have been trying to elude him. From then on, what follows in the four *Ring* operas is a complete joy, a totally unforgettable experience of more than sixteen hours' duration.

The year 2006 will show seven Wagner operas, the four of *The Ring* plus the *Flying Dutchman, Tristan und Isolde*, and *Parsifal*. A *Ring* production lasts four seasons, and in the fifth and sixth seasons, there is no *Ring*, in which case only three non-*Ring* operas are staged. This means that a new production takes place every six years.

The Bayreuth schedule in 2006 is as follows:

July 25	*The Flying Dutchman*
July 26	*Rhinegold*
July 27	*Valkyrie*
July 28	*No opera. Brünnhilde needs rest.*
July 29	*Siegfried*
July 30	*No opera. Brünnhilde and Siegfried need rest.*
July 31	*Twilight of the Gods*
August 1	*Tristan and Isolde*
August 2	*Parsifal*

This cycle will be repeated until the end of August, usually the twenty-eighth, when the festival will end with *Parsifal*. Note that in 2005, there was applause at the end of each act of *Parsifal* and at the end of the opera—something that was not done some years ago. I don't know from where the custom arose that there was not supposed to be applause in *Parsifal*. (Was it Wagner's recommendation? Or Cosima's? God knows!) Be as it may, that tradition is no longer being observed. People also applauded after *Parsifal* in New York, Berlin, and Cologne.

Tickets and accommodations for Bayreuth. When you decide to go to Bayreuth, there are two points you have to work way ahead of time. Tickets are the main thing, of course, then accommodations. In 1999, it cost somewhere around U$5,000, including air tickets.

Tickets. It is very difficult to get tickets to attend Bayreuth. There is a ten-year waiting list to obtain a ticket. The system works as follows: You write a letter to the ticket office, Bayreuther Festspiele Kartenbüro (box office), Postfach 10 02 62, D-95402, Bayreuth, Germany, requesting a ticket. You must indicate full address, phone(s), and the general price range desired. Tickets can be as high as 300 euros per opera. E-mail requests are accepted. That letter has to arrive between October 1 and October 15, neither before nor after those dates, of the year before the summer you wish to attend. You will ask for one ticket; however, two people with the same address may request two tickets. Then, sometime soon afterward, you will receive a letter from the Festspielhaus regretting they cannot provide your request. Try again, and you try next October, and on the tenth year, you will get a ticket for one Wagner opera, the one they decide on, on the date they decide. A German friend of mine told me that after writing for ten years, she got a ticket for *Parsifal*; she started writing again for a second ticket, and ten years later, she got one, and guess what? A ticket for *Parsifal!* I don't think that will occur today in the age of computers, but it has happened! On the day of the performance, there may be some leftover tickets, which are sold in the morning at the box office. It is not rare to find some person trying to get rid of tickets right before the opera starts. In general, Bayreuth doesn't approve of this situation. Tickets should be returned to the box office way ahead of time.

The total price of the tickets might be around 1,500 euros, not the best tickets, and some Wagner Associations add a surcharge to get your tickets for Bayreuth.

Tours. If you are traveling with a tour, of course, they will provide everything for you: tickets, accommodation, restaurants, tourist attractions, etc., and visits to tourist attractions in and out of town. You can find some tours listed in the opera magazines of London, Paris, and in *Opera News* (the magazine of the Metropolitan Opera in New York). I have traveled with some tours:

Dailey Thorp Travel (USA) (www.daileythorp.com/ mtdailey@wyoming.com);

Morgan Tours (Canada) (www.morgantours.com/ travel@morgantours.com);

Great Performance Tours (NY) (www.greatperformancetours.com/ jlazarus@mswtravelny.com).

And I strongly recommend them; they are all very good and efficient but can be expensive.

Wagner Associations. There are Wagner Associations in most large cities in the world. If you join one of them, it could be a way you can be helped to get a ticket; not guaranteed though. But they usually request and get a number of tickets for the use of their members. They will usually raffle the few tickets they get among those interested in going to Bayreuth. You can think of joining the Friends of Bayreuth, a highly paid membership, which can probably help you get tickets. Membership is about $500 a year.

Internet. After having reviewed all the possibilities, I think the best way is to join a tour. But if you are going on your own, you can look in Internet for accommodations in Bayreuth, or your travel agent can help.

Accommodations. There are three-, four-, and five-star hotels; there are inns, pensions, and even families can rent a room. A hotel, not four or five stars, but comfortable, may be 120 euros a night. I know of a family inn owned by Herr Klaus, which has small and comfortable single and double rooms, with baths and showers in the room. It has a plentiful breakfast buffet and a small restaurant for lunch and dinner. It is called Gasthof zum Brandenburger, St.-Georgen-9-95448 Bayreuth, telephone 0921/789060, fax 0921/78906240. The inn is located within walking distance from the train station, and the bus passes by the street on schedule.

A whole cycle may last ten days when there's a *Ring*; if you don't have tickets for a given opera, you may travel to nearby cities, like Nuremberg, Bamberg, and others.

How to get there. Fly to any of the large capitals—London, Paris, Berlin—or other cities, Frankfurt, and then change to Nuremberg, the nearby city. There are trains that leave for Bayreuth practically every half an hour or less, or you can take a taxi, which can take about half an hour, and cost some US$ 100 in 2001—it should be more now. You arrive at the train station in Bayreuth where there is a taxi line and a bus station so that you can easily get to your destination.

Attire. The attire is formal—black tie for men, long dresses for women—although many women come in short skirts and pants nowadays but not jeans, Reebok, or Adidas shoes.

Schedules. Operas often begin at 4:00 p.m. or 6:00 p.m., depending on their length. They usually last around five hours. *Rhinegold* is the shortest one. If you came in a tour, usually by 2:00 pm, everybody is dressed up in the hotel lobby, standing around the table consuming champagne, fruit punch, grapes, and cookies, which will help you through the first act of the opera. You might be able to hide some grapes in your purse, to munch at intermission, but no brown bags, please. If you are on your own, be sure you contact a taxi way ahead of time to come and pick you up at your hotel at 2:00 p.m. After that, all the taxis are busy.

You may walk from the center of town to the Festspielhaus; it takes about thirty minutes or take the bus (ask in your hotel or inn). If you are staying for the entire *Ring*, or for several days, be sure to contract your taxis for so many days and for such and such a time.

If you arrive early at the Fiestspielhaus, you will do as others do: parade around the beautiful gardens, look at the beautiful people, take photographs, etc. The start of the performance will be announced from the balcony somewhere in the second floor by a group of trumpets that will air a well-known leitmotif from the opera of the day. This routine will be repeated at the beginning of each act. Then the people begin moving slowly into the House. Because the theater is built as a horseshoe, with no aisles, people will be coming in and stand in front of their seats until the entire row is filled. By the second day, you know that you have to come early so that your neighbors won't look at you disapprovingly.

It is important to note that there is no playbill in Bayreuth. You buy a single-page item that announces the opera of the day: cast, all the collaborators, and then dates when this opera has been played in Bayreuth. There is no synopsis of the opera whatsoever. It seems that if you are here in Bayreuth, it is because you know your Wagner.

The acts last about one hour, usually more; the intermissions last one hour. *The Rhinegold*, a one-act opera (no intermission) lasts over two hours. The first act of *The Twilight of the Gods* lasts over two hours. There are no titles in Bayreuth. There is no applause within the acts, and there may be some at the end of the acts; but there is no applause at the end of *Parsifal*. This is changing.

Everybody has to come out of the House at the end of each act to let the building air out since there is no air-conditioning. The theater is small—about two thousand wooden seats, with wooden floors. Stumping on the floor is a common occurrence at the end of a performance, and of course, there will be applause or even booing.

Weather. At this point, it is important to comment on the Bayreuth weather. It is very changeable: it may be sunny in the morning, but when you come out at the first intermission, it may be cloudy and cool, and even humid. You better have a scarf somewhere to protect your throat.

If you get a sore throat, I strongly recommend that you go to a pharmacy and buy a German medicine called Mallebrin, a compound to gargle, which will cure you right away. Buy more than one little bottle so that you can bring it home and use it for your grandchildren. Another thing, buy some lozenges or cough drops to avoid dryness of the throat and that coughing that may hit you at any time when least expected. Anybody who dares to make a noise is looked at very disapprovingly. Disaster! You would wish the earth will swallow you.

Intermissions. Coming out at intermission, people move out to the side of the vendors of sausages, beer, ice cream, wine, pretzels, etc. There is a cafeteria with a very wide variety of delicious dishes and cakes, etc.; there are several luxurious restaurants where you make the reservations to obtain a complete dinner before the opera starts, to dine at both intermissions (the first course in the first intermission, and the main course and dessert at the second intermission)—an expensive enterprise, of course. You will need to make a reservation before the opera, as in all the theaters of the world.

At intermission, you congregate with your friends to comment about the opera, and in groups, you move about to get some food.

There is a book-and-record shop anywhere in the garden; crowds will gather there, and you can buy Bayreuth commemorative mail stamps and dispatch your mail right from the post office there. Many such cards never arrive to their destination because the stamps are so beautiful and valuable that they get "stopped" somewhere along their way. You can buy all kinds of souvenirs and, above all, buy the yearly book of Bayreuth—a gigantic book that contains many articles of interest in three languages and details of the operas of the year.

After the performance, your tour bus will take you back to your hotel, or if you are on your own, you can pick up a bus to the train station, or you can walk there, where there are buses and taxis to take you home. I usually stayed by the parking lot after the performance to see the singers coming out and obtain photographs and autographs. By the time all this was done, the last bus to the train station had long passed, so I had to walk alone or with other autograph seekers. There, at the convenience store, I bought some cookies, fruit, tea, or whatever and took a taxi to the inn. Munching on this food, I would reminisce about the opera just seen and think about the opera of the next day.

What to do in Bayreuth during the morning? Most people get up very leisurely and have a plentiful breakfast at their hotel or inn. Then they go out to the streets, as do all tourists in the world.

They walk along the cobbled streets of the town, pass by, or stop to listen to the groups of young musicians from Germany and other countries, who play classical music in the corners, and later pass the hat. All the people will sit comfortably under the umbrellas of the street cafes, and some may start drinking beer, even before lunch. You can buy food from the street vendors.

It is very picturesque to see youngsters in bicycles carrying a small cardboard sign that reads, "Suche Karten" ("Looking for a ticket").

But beware, there are Wagner activities going on in the mornings. Singers may appear in the record—or bookstores, signing autographs, selling records or videos. You will be surprised at the very large number of books about Wagner in German, which never get translated into English. The daily newspaper will bring a daily review of the opera, and you will enjoy reading and commenting with your friends to enhance your knowledge about the opera.

More important than all that's said above, there are conferences in the mornings, especially on the occasion of *The Ring*. These are paid events. I know and have attended the one series of conferences offered by the Wagner Society of New York in English, which provides musical examples from CD recordings, and there is another series given in German by a world-known young German pianist Stefan Mickish, who has paraphrased many of Wagner's operas. He presents musical examples played by him on the piano. He usually sells his recordings at the end of the conference.

Another event that takes place in the morning is the visit to the Theater. The tour is a paid event. You will be taken down to see the rooms of storage of all the paraphernalia of the operas being shown and many items of the theater; then the costume rooms, the sewing rooms, where many seamstresses are working; the wig room; the room of shoes; and other items. Then you come to the pit of the orchestra. Notice the relative position of the conductor to the musicians; the latter are seated in rows arranged not in a plane but in an inclined plane. Apparently, it is very difficult to conduct in Bayreuth, so expressed Pierre Boulez when he came to conduct the centenary *Ring* in 1976. Having paraded through the innards of the Theater will give you a special feeling when you are seated up above, watching the opera.

Wahnfried. In the mornings, you can also tour the city of Bayreuth and visit Wagner's house—Wahnfried (Peace from Illusion)—to where he moved in 1873. It is within walking distance from the center of town. There is an entrance fee. Some events, like recitals, take place at Wahnfried during the mornings. There is no guided tour; you walk the place on your own. There is the main room, which houses Wagner's library and his piano; there is a room dedicated to Venice memorabilia; in the corridors, you will see glass cases that contain Wagner's costumes—silk robes, hats, boots, etc. He was a short man, judging by the size of the costumes. There are many corridors covered with photographs of Wagner's productions in Bayreuth. There is a model of the orchestra in the sunken pit, where you can observe and understand how the orchestra is placed under the stage. At the end, there is a room with chairs where they are continuously showing Wagner's videos. You can relax there while you watch the operas. Wagner is buried in the garden of this house; so is Cosima and their dog. There are always fresh flowers in the graves—fans bring them to them.

Bayreuth by night. There are some evening events in Bayreuth, usually on nights when there is no opera. For example, there are recitals by the singers. Also, singing is done at churches and at Sunday mass (http://www.bayreuther-festspiele.de/Anfangsseite/deutsch.htm).

Experiences. There is a great moment I remember from Bayreuth. I went there for the first time in the summer of 1995. I saw the seven operas of the season. One such was *Tristan and Isolde*; the first time I saw it, the production was by Heiner Müller. Eric Wonder was the stage director, and the sets recalled the painters of Rothko in ochre colors, and costumes were by Yohji Yamamoto. The conductor was Daniel Barenboim, and the singers were Waltraud Meier and Siegfried Jerusalem. At the end of the third act (end of opera), Isolde sings the *Liebestod* (death by love) after Tristan has died. Ms. Meier got up from where she was on the floor next to Tristan and walked to the center front of the stage where she began to sing:

Isolde: Isolde:
How gently and quietly   *Mild und leise*
he smiles,   *wie er lächelt,*
how fondly   *wie das Auge*
he opens his eyes!   *hold er öffnet—*

From then on, I felt like as if I was levitating because Wagner's music starts at one level, and Isolde urges you to rise and come up and up with her feelings; one feels short of breath, totally immersed in the music. She continues singing, inebriated by fragrances:

Isolde:

In the surging swell,
in the ringing sound,
in the vast wave
of the world's breath—
to drown,
to sink
unconscious—
supreme bliss!

She was wearing a fur coat when she came to center stage, but she let it drop off her shoulders when she started to sing. Now the ray of light encircled her; her dress was at one moment a metallic silver, at others shimmering gold. When she finished singing, there was a long, long, long silence. The audience had been transported to the realms Isolde was asking us to follow her, so we had not returned to reality as yet. It took a bit of time, and after that silence, which appeared to be eternal, the applause exploded—the feet stumping on the wooden floor, cheers, bravos, etc. This lasted for some twenty minutes or more. The singers kept coming out over and over again until finally the iron curtain of the stage was lowered, and people knew it was time to leave. That has been the greatest artistic experience I have ever been exposed to, just as when I saw Maria Callas on stage.

In another opportunity, in the summer of 1999, I was again in Bayreuth to see the same production of *Tristan*. This time, my friend Lucy from Paris had come along, but she did not have tickets for the operas. I let her use my *Tristan* ticket to enter and see the second act; I had seen the first act and would go in again for the third act. People moved into the theater for the second act, and I remained seated on a bench in one of the corridors—there was not a soul around. Then, from the end of the corridor, there appeared Mr. Wolfgang Wagner (Wagner's grandson and director of the Bayreuth Festival). He asked me why I was there, and I explained. He said I was not allowed to be there once the opera had started. He asked me to follow him, which I did. He took me through a door to the stairway leading to the balcony of the House. At the standing of the stairs, there was a red velvet curtain, which he opened, and showed me to get in. There it was, a small cozy room, with red velvet seats, and he told me that was the room where the Wagner family sat when they came to a performance. Cosima had her own box up in the second floor at the center of the House. I sat quietly, alone in that room, and saw the second act of *Tristan*. It was the last *Tristan* of the twentieth century in Bayreuth. My friend could not believe my luck when I told her my experience. She was not lucky, though—she had to sit in a bench in the garden throughout the third act of *Tristan*.

Type of audience. I would like to comment on the type of audience who attends the Ring Festival in Bayreuth. There are many older people, some of who have been coming for years, always to the same hotel room and/or the same inn—very proper, they move slowly, quietly. Nobody is in a rush, and there is a quality of restraint in this crowd (fashion trendy). Many Japanese women wear their luxurious exotic kimonos, and for some reason, it appears that the Japanese are the only ones prepared with small cushions for the seats and backs of the wooden chairs of the theater. The older crowd knows very well the theater, the surrounding areas, the restaurants, etc.

Then there are the middle-aged people; a little more mobile, they move in throngs to the vendors, without running, though; many will sit with their friends at a cafeteria table to discuss the opera act they just saw.

There are less young people. It must be because of the price of the tickets.

Many Wagner Associations of the world bring some of their members to Bayreuth every year, so when you are walking around, you may be able to meet and greet people from the Wagner Society of New York or Los Angeles, San Diego, Barcelona (Spain), Montreal, Paris, Caracas, and many others. If you have come more than once, you may find familiar faces.

Other Ring Festivals. I have never attended a Ring Festival in Salzburg but have been to other summer festivals. Salzburg is probably more fashion conscious, and again, older people predominate, and possibly more younger people are seen here every year. But Bayreuth is more festive because of the beautiful gardens where people stroll.

Berlin and New York are less trendy, more informal; you may find some people with bundles in New York; that is because they spend all day out shopping or something, and then at night, they come to the theater. But when there is a Ring Festival, everybody is up to their best finery.

It is interesting to note that very many foreign Wagner lovers come to those festivals. They may make up about 50 percent of the audience at Bayreuth and a very high number in Berlin, New York, or Cologne.

The Covent Garden and old Paris theaters—Chatelet, Bastille, Palais Garnier, and Champs Elysees—are all informal; but of course, it depends on where you are sitting. But the terrible spectacle of youngsters in jeans, with backpacks and Reebok shoes, is very common and disgusting. They don't feel any respect for the opera, and, of course, they probably do not know better.

What I am going to write about next is very disagreeable. The most terrible experience I have ever had in my years of opera going, everywhere, comes from Covent Garden and Opera Garnier in Paris. That experience was having the dirtiest people in the world sitting right next to me. The theater should have a placard somewhere in a visible area that reads, "Please, take a bath and change your clothing and socks before you come to the opera. That way, you will not offend your seat neighbors. Everybody has the right to watch the performance without intermingling smells of dirty jeans, salami, marijuana, cigarette butts, beer, sweat, and the like. Be respectful and, above all, clean." As I said, the matter is very disagreeable, but it is true. It may happen to you too.

Recordings and videos. If you are interested in recordings and videos of *The Ring*, search in the Internet for Amazon.com. For recordings, also check the Schwann catalogue. There are several complete Bayreuth *Ring*s recorded from 1952, 1953, 1956, 1957, and 1958 with very good casts and different conductors. From this period is the 1955 *Ring*, the first complete *Ring* live stereo recording from Bayreuth, previously unpublished, conducted by Joseph Keildberth, now being released in 2006 by Testament (London). This *Ring* features Astrid Varnay (Brünnhilde), Hans Hotter (Wotan), and Ramón Vinay (Siegfried).

An historical complete recording is the one produced by John Culshaw, which was the first recorded *Ring* in a studio. It was started in 1958 and ended in 1965; it was digitally remastered in 1984. It was conducted by Georg Solti with the Vienna Philarmonic Orchestra for Decca Record Company Limited, London. The cast features famous singers like Kirsten Flagstaad (Fricka), who now, at the end of her career as a soprano, has taken this mezzo role in *Rhinegold*; Birgit Nilsson (Brünnhilde); Regine Krispin (Sieglinde); Christa Ludwig (Fricka); Lucia Popp and Gywneth Jones (Rhinemadens) who later on became a famous Brünnhilde, as in the centenary production of Boulez-Chéreau in 1976. This recording also features Joan Sutherland as the forest bird, who, in spite of terrible diction, became one of the best sopranos of the twentieth century. She once said, "People don't come to hear my words; they come to listen to my voice." And that was true.

Bayreuth live radio broadcast. This is the last of my revelations about the Wagner Festival in Bayreuth. The festival comes live every year directly from Bayreuth through Radio Bavaria. The first cycle is broadcast in its entirety from the twenty-fifth of July to August 2 (when there are seven operas); then the operas continue to be rebroadcast through different radio stations at different schedules. The Web address in 2006 is http://www.operacast.com/bayreuth06.htm#hollander.

The cast for the 2006 *Ring* is practically all new to me. I only know very few of those singers: Falk Struckmann, who is the Wotan, whom I first heard in 1995 when he was Kurvenal in *Tristan und Isolde*, and again in 1999; Linda Watson (Brünnhilde), heard as Elsa in Lohengrin in 2000 and 2001; and Korean bass baritone Kwangchui Youn (Fassolt) who has performed this role before in Bayreuth. Bayreuth makes singers; for instance, many singers of *The Ring*, like the Valkyries and the Rhinemaidens, come young and not very famous, but after having being four years in *The Ring*, the doors of many opera houses in the world will open to them. Some of them will become Waltrautes or even Brünnhildes, and the Waltrautes may become Frickas, and others will end performing the heralds and flower maidens in *Parsifal*, as well as in some Mozart operas.

In the case of the male roles, usually the singers are well seasoned because the male characters in *The Ring* have difficult music to sing; and strong voices are required—like Wotan, Alberich, and Hagen—and others require a lot of acting like Loge and Mime. Both of these characters need some acting, which has to convey some comic elements and scheming, and somehow, the voice has to be altered. Siegfried's character requires a voice with stamina and style since the Siegfried of *Siegfried* is different from the one in the *Twilight*. *The Ring* of 2006 is produced by Tankred Dorst, with set design by Frank Philipp Schlössmann, and conducted by Chrstian Thielmann, a German musician who has conducted previously in Bayreuth. It is a picturesque moment to see when the full orchestra appears on stage to take curtain call after the complete performance of *The Ring* and at the end of each complete cycle. The orchestra is made up of very good musicians, many of them young, who are recruited very rigorously from other orchestras and from music schools in Germany and Europe. They appear in jeans, T-shirts, shorts, and what-have-you, even the conductor. It is too hot down in the pit, so they dress accordingly.

There are some videos of the complete *Ring*, possibly in DVDs, nowadays. Chronologically: (1) the centenary production by Patrice Chéreau and conducted by Pierre Boulez, with John Mc Intyre (Wotan), Hanna Schwarz (Fricka), Jeannine Altmeier (Sieglinde), Peter Hoffmann (Siegmund), Gwyneth Jones (Brünnhilde), and Siegfried Jerusalem (Siegfried). This production is from Bayreuth (1979-80); (2) the Harry Kupfer production (Bayreuth, 1988) conducted by Daniel Barenboim with Jon Tomlinson (Wotan), Linda Finnie (Fricka), Anne Evans (Brünnhilde), and Siegfried Jerusalem (Siegfried); (3) the Metropolitan production by Otto Schenk with Janmes Morris (Wotan), Hanna Schwarz (Fricka), Placido Domingo (Siegmund), Jessye Norman (Siegliende), Hildergard Behrens (Brünnhilde), and Siegfried Jerusalem (Siegfried). Both records and videos of the isolated operas exist. Bayreuth does not usually produce videos; they consider it a very expensive enterprise, and there is no guarantee that they may be commercially successful.

By now, you know a lot about Bayreuth. When you get to the festival, from the moment you arrive at the gardens of the Festspielhaus, try to pin your experience to what it means to be there. Think of Wagner who built the theater and all of his efforts to have it constructed. Of all the time he spent rehearsing *The Ring*, he himself at the piano, and directing the production with somebody taking notes of which a book was published. While you sit waiting for *Rhinegold* to start, think how it must have been on the night of the premiere of *The Ring* on August 13, 1876. That way, you will tie your experience with an historical *Ring*. It is said that people come to Bayreuth by plane, train, car, or even bicyccle; but the real Wagnerite comes on his knees.

The premiere. The premiere of *The Ring* from August 13-17, 1876, was the greatest artistic event in the last quarter of the nineteenth century in Europe.

There was great expectation in the cultural world about this event. Wagner had been working very hard for years to build the theater and had traveled much to conduct and give recitals in different countries in Europe to collect money for his project and had organized groups of patrons who contributed highly with funds. When the time came, everybody who was anybody was there: king Pedro II of Brazil and the king of Portugal, princes, poets, writers, painters, architects, musicians, conductors, all the Russian composers; all the European and Russian elite was there; and, of course, all the patrons from all the European countries and even America. Nothing of that sort had occurred before, and, of course, the Tetralogy was a tremendous success. Wagner was already very famous and considered to be the most influential artist of his time. That was the only presentation of *The Ring* in Bayreuth in the nineteenth century under the direction of Hans Richter.

There is an account of this event by Pyotr Ilyich Tchaikovsky (7) who was present. He spends some of his narration referring to the fact that the town ran out of food. Neither bread nor beer could be found, much less any other type of food; such was the multitude that turned up for the premiere. He thought it was great.

The next presentation of an opera in Bayreuth was the premiere of *Parsifal* (26 July 1882) under the direction of Hermann Levi. Wagner traveled to Venice in September of that year, and he died there on the thirteenth of February 1883. He was buried in Bayreuth on February 18.

Wagner and Nietzsche. Famous among the famous present at the premiere of *The Ring* was Frederich Nietzsche, Wagner's best friend. They had met in 1868 when Nietzsche was twenty-four years old and rapidly established a very deep friendship. He had attended the rehearsals of *The Ring*, but when the event came, he became seriously appalled and disgusted with what he saw. He thought the festival had been like a big market fair celebration, with adoring patrons surrounding the master and he, Wagner, entertaining them; he, the true friend, was left aside. He began to distance himself from Wagner and began to criticize his music, art, and works. By the time *Parsifal* came along in 1882, he had totally separated from Wagner. Their friendship possibly caused much constraint on Nietzsche, and he began to liberate himself from the domineering attitude of Wagner. They had always had conversations about Greek art and drama, and Nietzsche was able to mature his ideas for his first book, *The Birth of Tragedy*.

Nietzsche criticized *Parsifal* because he thought that Wagner was emulating Christianity in the opera by representing high Christian rituals, though Wagner was not a Christian. He thus considered him to be a fake. Nietzsche hated Christianity; his ideal was the Superman, no God involved. Nietzsche wrote two books against Wagner. *The Wagner Case* and *Nietzsche Contra Wagner*.

When Wagner died, they had not seen each other for some time. All in all, *The Ring* has reigned in art since its first complete presentation to the world in 1876.

BIBLIOGRAPHY

1. Lattimore, Richmond. 1951. *The Iliad of Homer*. Chicago: Chicago University Press.

2. Porter, Andrew. 1976. *The Ring of the Nibelung*. London: WW Norton & Co.

3. Newman, Ernest. 1982. *El Hombre y el Artista*. Madrid: Taurus Edition SA.

4. *L'Or du Rhin*. 1992. L'Avant Scène. bimonthly. Paris: Editions Premières Loges Table I.

5. Wagner, Richard. 1993. *My Life* (Autobiographical Sketch in *Art and Revolution*), p. 65. Nebraska: Nebraska Univesity Press.

6. Buller, Jeffrey. 2001. *Classically Romantic: Classical Form and Meaning in Wagner's Ring*. Philadelphia: Xlibris Corp.

7. Sutcliffe, Tom. ed. 2002. *The Faber Book of Opera* London: Faber & Faber Ltd.: 319-29.

8. Lee, Fr. M. Owen. 2003. *Athena Sings: Wagner and the Greeks*. Canada: Univesity of Toronto Press Inc.

9. Björnsson, Árni. 2003. *Wagner and Volsungs*. London: University College of London.

NOTE

Figures 1-4. Drawings by Morella Pinto Rondón.

Figures 6-9. Wagner's Museum near Dresden. Photos by author.

Figure 10. Photo by member of AWV.

THE END

Teresa Rondon Rota

May 22, 2006 on the 103d anniversary of my mother's birth (1903-1998), on the 124th anniversary of Wagner's birth (1813-1883), and on my eightieth birthday.

INDEX

Printed in Great Britain
by Amazon.co.uk, Ltd.,
Marston Gate.